LOUISIANA STATE UNIVERSITY STUDIES
Max Goodrich, General Editor

Humanities Series
Donald E. Stanford, Editor

Number Eighteen
Explorations of Literature

Explorations
of
Literature

Edited by
Rima Drell Reck

Louisiana State University Press
BATON ROUGE
MCMLXVI

PREFACE

THIS COLLECTION of essays by the members of the Department of English and Speech and the Department of Foreign Languages at Louisiana State University in New Orleans is representative of the richness and diversity of literary and critical interests of this young faculty. Including structural studies and literary history, stylistic analyses and examinations of symbolic patterns, tracing of comparative themes and delineation of aesthetic theories, these essays range in approach and are illustrative of the eclectic nature of literary scholarship in the United States today. The topics are as varied as the critical methods. One essay deals with the theory of modern drama. In the field of English literature, there are studies of Gower, Shakespeare, Milton, Shelley, and Conrad. In American literature, Melville, Fitzgerald, and Dos Passos are examined. In the area of foreign literature, the authors consider the Mexican Modernists, Carmontelle, Baudelaire, and Flaubert.

This volume was made possible by the interest and cooperation of my colleagues at Louisiana State University in New Orleans. I wish also to express my thanks to Professor Donald E. Stanford for suggesting the volume and for his encouragement in its preparation.

R. D. R.

CONTENTS

Explorations of Literature

AUGUST W. STAUB

FROM IBSEN TO KAISER:
THE SUBJECTIVE PERSPECTIVE

THERE ARE THOSE who revel in it and those who despair of it. There are those who are militant about it and those who wearily pray for some rational deliverance from its ever increasing decadence. But whether we consider ourselves victims or fortunate heirs, there is no denying that we are the latest participants in the Romantic revolution that began more than a century and a half ago. Moreover, only history will tell whether we are the last of a long line of revolutionaries or simply another generation of contributors to a movement whose end is still nowhere in sight.

If one wished, a case could probably be presented for the emergence of a new classicism. In contemporary poetry, for instance, there is the voice of such a man as Yvor Winters, who calls out for a return to the discipline, restraint, and rational decorum of classical standards. But however strong the evidence for a shift towards classicism, we must have reservations about the conclusions it invites. This is especially true in terms of the theater, where there have been a number of false alarms in the recent past. Realism, for example, was heralded as the death knell of Romanticism. But hardly had Realism become established than it was faced with a counterrevolution in the form of German Expressionism, a movement which Nicoll describes as "modern classicism."[1] It now seems, however, that we have gained a sufficiently long retrospective advantage to be able to say with assurance that, however different either of these movements

3

may have been from each other, they both had one thing in common: they were both equally romantic.

This is an important fact to recognize, for it gives us a distinct critical advantage over those who are still busily and somewhat pointlessly engaged in separating and describing one or another of the many literary and artistic "isms" of the past seventy or eighty years. We are able to do what they cannot: disentangle ourselves from the confusing little pet hates and loves of each of the "isms" and view all of the modern arts as parallel expressions of common romantic ideals and philosophies. Moreover, the time is ripe for such an approach. When one is caught up in the vortex of a new and exciting art movement, one has neither the time nor, above all, the inclination to rob the new endeavor of its luster by emphasizing its similarities with developments in the other contemporary arts. But that day is long past. The storm in modern art and literature has long since been over. Van Gogh now hangs over the fireman's mantel. Picasso is a very old and very rich man. It has been more than seventy years since Nora closed that all-important door to the *Doll's House,* and both *Ulysses* and *Lady Chatterly's Lover* have finally managed to elude the vigilance of those praiseworthy and staunch protectors of public innocence—the United States postal and customs officials. In short, only the ignorant and the naïve can fail to realize that the avant-garde has exchanged places with the academy and that we now stand near the end of a virtually complete artistic era. In terms of the critic, ours is indeed a fortunate position, for we are now able to view with a relatively unjaundiced eye the totality of that movement in arts and letters which we have termed "modern."

What we see from our vantage point is an all-pervading, anti-intellectual Romanticism, a Romanticism whose beginnings are buried somewhere in the late eighteenth century but whose distinctly modern manifestations can be traced to the last quarter of the nineteenth century. It was at that time that the growing forces of modernism culminated in a widespread burst of intellectual and artistic activity which revolutionized contemporary thinking and gave birth to such philosophers and artists as Nietzsche, Ibsen, Flaubert, Zola, Henry and William James, Strindberg, and Freud. Different as each of these men was, they all had a common romantic heritage; and from it they fashioned a new and distinctly modern philosophy. To begin with, each had a sacred reverence for the importance of the private individual, such a reverence that they were prompted to develop what LeSage calls the "cult of the ego."[2] Essentially, this meant that truth, as they saw it, was an irrational, subjective phenomenon. Truth was, in Nietzschean terms, Dionysian not Apollonian. In other words, the ego did not exist in the world; the world existed in and for the ego. Stated in terms of the arts, the cult of the ego invites the following comparison with more classical standards: Classicism's genius lay in the artist's ability to make the subject serve the object; modern Romanticism's genius lies in the artist's manipulation of the object in order to serve the subject.

This passionate interest in the worth and value of the individual soul led to the development of yet another important tenet of modern thought—the belief in a relative moral standard. The absolute morality of an earlier day was discarded and in its place was set a sliding yardstick of values which changed with each new individual and each new set of circumstances. This total acceptance of relativism is to Joseph Wood Krutch the very thing which characterizes modernism. In his comments on *An Enemy of the People*, Krutch states that "at last we have reached something that, for the first time, might justify talk about a chasm separating the past from the future."

A new world which has come to accept an all-inclusive relativity actually would not be merely different from, it would be genuinely discontinuous with an old one, in which on the whole, it was assumed that some unchanging principles existed.[3]

Just how and why the concepts of moral relativism and anti-intellectual subjectivism came to be established as the twin beacons of modern thought is an intriguing story, but one which need not be told here. It is more to the point at hand that the two concepts existed as sufficiently important and widespread ideals to be recognized as synonyms for all that was most modern in artistic and scientific thought. To the artists of the late nineteenth and early twentieth centuries, the problem was not whether the two ideas were philosophically acceptable—that was a foregone conclusion—but rather how they were to be given adequate artistic expression. To solve this problem called for new forms and techniques; and, thus, the early modern artists set out feverishly on voyages of discovery.

The history of the modern movements in art is, above all, a history
of an adventure in new forms.

In literature, for instance, there was the development of the
modern psychological novel. What makes this novel form modern is
not its interest in psychology per se, for all novelists have been
interested in human psychology, but rather its relentless pursuit of
new techniques for rendering that psychology, that is, new modes
of subjectively presenting the individual in the light of relativistic
values. The most important of these new techniques centered themselves around the convention best equipped to join issue with an
all-inclusive subjective relativism. That convention was the manipulation of the first person subjective point of view.

As early as Richardson's use of the epistolary method, and even
before, there had been some effort on the part of the novelist to tell
his story from a first person point of view, but the history of the novel
up until the last years of the nineteenth century is primarily the
story of the development and exploitation of the method of omniscient narration. Most of the great nineteenth-century novelists were
happy to retain the neo-classic advantage of knowing and seeing all
and of being able to break into their story with authorial comment
whenever they felt the urge or need. The modern novelist, however,
soon realized that it was not only difficult but anachronistic to express a relative world view in a form which based its argument on
notions of absolutism and universality. Thus, such novelists as Zola
abandoned the omniscient approach for the quasi-scientific quality of
the third person objective point of view. Presently, the restrictions
of this objectivity became oppressive to those who wished to make
a more subjective statement; and in consequence they turned to
experiments with the rendition of first person subjective viewpoints.

Chief among the early practitioners of the first person method was
Henry James, brother of the noted modern relativist, William James.
Crying out that he wished to "dramatize, dramatize," Henry James
began to flirt with the telling of complete stories through the subjective perception of one or more of the characters participating directly
in the action of the tale. Among his many experiments with varying
points of view are such familiar works as *The Turn of the Screw*
and *Wings of the Dove*. In the former, James presented his tale
solely through the point of view of the central character, and so
rigorously did he hold himself to her viewpoint that a violent critical

controversy still continues to be waged about what actually took place in the action of the story. In *Wings of the Dove* James's method was to present several different points of view, each serving as a reflector of the other. The value of the Jamesian method to a subjective relativist is too obvious to need extended comment. Such a technique shifts the emphasis from the intrigue of the plot to the actions of the character's subjective ego; and in doing this it forces the reader, willing or not, into an empathic response, which, in turn, makes the reader regard the character in terms of relative, not absolute, moral standards.

Since James was always the novelist of the human consciousness, his presentation of point of view remained on, or close to, the level of the organizing intelligence. As the century drew to a close, however, the rise of Freudian psychology, with its emphasis on the barely conscious and the metaconscious levels of psychic activity, forced a change in the history of the novel. More and more the novelist became interested in the secret truth locked in the murky recesses of the ego. Thus, in 1913 Proust published the first volumes of a new kind of study in point of view. *Remembrances of Things Past* was a more or less autobiographical investigation of that intermediate level of psychic activity which lies between the intellect on the one hand and the subconscious on the other, the level which has come to be known as the "stream of consciousness." What Proust invited the reader to do was to watch along with him as he observed the flood of images bubbling up from below and passing on into the stream of consciousness. Within ten years, what Proust had done autobiographically, James Joyce was to extend to characters totally alien to the author. In 1922 there appeared *Ulysses*, a novel which presented the points of view of several characters as seen through their respective streams of consciousness. Thereafter, the problem was stated and the path cleared for the many, many good and bad studies in point of view which give to the contemporary novel its modernity. Here is not the place to pursue the matter any further. Suffice it to say that the modern novelist had found in the convention of first person subjective point of view the structural mode which best suited his desire to state an ego-centered, relativistic philosophy. But what of the other arts? Can we draw a parallel? The answer is a decided "yes," for their story is surprisingly similar to that of the novel, though many specialists, locked within the narrow confines of their own particular area of interest, have failed to recognize the similarity. This is especially true of the students of modern drama, and such a myopia has seriously hampered our critical insight.

Perhaps we are not totally to blame, for we have been warned off any serious consideration of the uses of point of view in drama by the somewhat jealous zeal of the critics of the novel and we have meekly accepted their pronouncements. In 1926, for instance, Percy Lubbock, in his very influential work *The Craft of Fiction*, stated that "the whole intricate question of method, in the craft of fiction, I take to be governed by the question of point of view."[4] In the following year, E. M. Forster's equally influential *Aspects of the Novel* contained the observation that "the problem of point of view certainly is peculiar to the novel."[5] Even as late as 1955, Leon Edel was saying that in *Strange Interlude* O'Neill was merely imitating James Joyce.[6]

Such arguments are unfounded. Modern painting, for example, offers strong evidence to the contrary. In Kandinsky's abstract landscapes the viewer is given a chromatic translation of the painter's stream of consciousness, and in the fantasies of Paul Klee we have a presentation of that same world of Jungian imagery that Joyce unearthed in the "Night Town" section of *Ulysses*. Moreover, Helen Gardner points out, a perfectly workable definition of cubism is an art style which presents "a succession of points of view, such as front, profile, and back, known to the mind but not seen by the eye simultaneously."[7] With such an interest evidenced by the visual arts in the issue of subjective points of view, it hardly seems likely that the drama, a form so closely akin to the novel, would have ignored the question entirely. And, indeed, such is not the case; the contrary is closer to the truth. Edel's accusation of O'Neill nowithstanding, there is every indication that the playwright's interest in point of view began just as early as that of the modern novelist; and there is strong support for the contention that dramatic experiments with point of view may have predated by a number of years some of the more important innovations of the novel.

To be fair, one must note that there are a few critics who have taken notice of this phenomenon. John Gassner, for instance, dismisses dramatic experiments with point of view as an impossible attempt to imitate the novel. Nicoll lists such experiments as one of many directions of modern drama. Alan Downer, in *The Art of the*

Play, devotes a brief chapter to point of view and the dramatic illusion. But nowhere is there a thorough treatment of the subject nor any indication that the issue of point of view may be considered the chief dramaturgic problem of modern playwriting, a problem which has occupied the attention of most of the modern masters including Ibsen, Strindberg, Kaiser, O'Neill, Pirandello, and Giraudoux. Most of the modern critics, having taken an "ism's"-eye view, have been too busy classifying works as realistic or symbolic, futuristic or grotesque, to realize that the great playwrights of the modern theater tend to transcend these narrow limits and to display an amazing similarity in themes and techniques. In fine, the great modern playwrights have been concerned with expressing a romantic, essentially irrational, relativistic world view; and, like the contemporary novelists, they have found their structural solution in the introduction of the first person point of view into the dramatic illusion.

The history of point of view methods in the drama parallels that of the novel and finds its beginnings in that famous contemporary of Henry James, the playwright Henrik Ibsen. Like all discussions of modern drama, this one will also return to the master, but its consideration of Ibsen will take a somewhat different path from the traditional. Ibsen was a great innovator, but not, perhaps, in the manner in which we normally view him. Traditionally, he is credited with the perfection of modern realism. This is true, but only if we carefully reassess our current concept of realism. For some time Ibsenian realism has been held up as the very antithesis of the French well-made play, but this view is no longer so easy to defend. From the advantage of more than seventy years, Ibsen appears much better costumed for the role of an irenic than for that of a St. George; that is, Ibsen now seems much more likely to be a savior than a destroyer of the well-made dragon. As Martin Lamm has commented, "In stating a problem, working out a plot, drawing a character, or writing dialogue, Ibsen was developing the technique of the French drama."[8]

What Ibsen did do was not to sound the death knell of the well-made play, but rather to introduce into it a sweeping structural change which attempted to bring the form into closer accord with his own relativistic philosophy. Prior to Ibsen, the dramatist, like the novelist, was an omniscient author. He reserved the right to see and know all and to comment on characters or present information directly to the audience. His chief means of doing this were the aside and the soliloquy, and Ibsen attacked both with great vigor. As early as the writing of *The League of Youth*, Ibsen boasts that he has accomplished "the feat of doing without a single monologue, without a single aside."[9] In other words, just as Zola and Flaubert did in the novel, Ibsen was consciously writing his plays from a third person objective point of view.

Thus it is that, above all else, Ibsen's so-called realism is actually the creation of an objectivity of structure which replaced the older formula of the omniscient dramatist. In doing what he did, Ibsen created the first broad direction of modern drama, which, if one desires, can be labeled externalism. It grew and prospered mightily, and its general good health has continued to the present day. Shake the bloom from the average Broadway hit, *Tea and Sympathy*, for instance, make a few small allowances for change in social customs, and one has the French well-made thesis play with its intrigue, its big curtains, and its pretentions, all decked out in the strait jacket of Ibsenian externalism. But for all its success, externalism is but a case of arrested development, for in reality it is only a stage in the progress of modern drama toward the more important business of rendering the dramatic illusion through the subjective viewpoint of the dramatic characters themselves. Externalism was, however, an important step, for it made playwrights aware of the inherent possibilities of point of view. As Alan Downer indicates: "Once the idea of point of view becomes established, once it becomes a tool, the playwright will experiment with its possibilities. The objectivity of the scientist, however highly touted as an ideal by Ibsen, Zola, and Chekhov, places unnatural restrictions on the creative mind."[10]

Ibsen himself realized this fact; and with the writing of *The Wild Duck* in 1884, he began casting about for a means to break through the barrier of third person objectivity. The method he elected to employ was symbolism, an interesting if not quite adequate one. To develop in detail the increasingly symbolic trend of Ibsen's middle and later work is beyond the scope of this paper. The significant point is that the trend indicated Ibsen's growing annoyance with externalism, and it represented his attempt to make a statement through the subjective viewpoints of his characters. Moreover, by a careful orchestration of all symbols so that they referred only to his heroine, he was able in *Hedda Gabler* to come surprisingly close to his subjective ideal; and it would not be amiss to say that Hedda is as consummate a point of view study as is Isabel in Henry James's *Portrait of a Lady*. Ibsen's accomplishments in this direction, however, were to go no further. The lead passed from him to his younger contemporary, August Strindberg.

Strindberg, who had made his fame as an externalistic playwright, suffered toward the end of the nineteenth century a severe mental collapse, which he himself characterized as his "inferno" period. During this time he wrote no plays, but harrowed, instead, the Swedenborgian hell. With the turn of the century, he emerged from this intensely mystical experience to startle the theatrical world with a number of strikingly unique works, chief among which were *The Dream Play* and *The Ghost Sonata*. The former play, which was his first consummate presentation of his new form, was written in 1901–1902. Space does not permit an extended study of its involved structural patterns, but it must be recognized as the earliest dramatic example of the use of the first person subjective point of view. In essence, the play is a rendering of the author's stream of consciousness in which images, rising unbidden from the subconscious, play upon it in weird and nightmarish patterns. Time and space are completely ignored, and external reality is present only through the vaguest of suggestions. What we have in *The Dream Play* is an autobiographical study of the playwright's mind operating in no larger sphere of action than the mind itself. This is the theatrical equivalent to the later soul-dredgings of Marcel Proust, and it predates by almost a quarter of a century the so highly admired "Night Town" section of *Ulysses*.

Strindberg's study of his own stream of consciousness was, within ten years, followed by the monodrama of the Russian playwright and director Nikolai Evreinov. Yet another step into the realm of dramatic presentation of the first person viewpoint, the monodrama was a rendering of external reality only in terms of the conflicts within an individual soul. It was not the drama of the interactions of men but the drama of the flux and reflux of a single soul. Evreinov argued that all the action of the play should be told through the viewpoint of a central character, since this was the truest possible statement of the notion that the objective world takes its animation from the moods of the subject. Thus, in his 1912 monodrama, *The Theatre of the Soul*, Evreinov sets the action in the heart of the central character; and the matter of the play is an argument between the various aspects of the central character's personality. As the quarrel proceeds, the two external characters of the play, the hero's wife and mistress, undergo surprising changes as the hero's internal conflict winds its shifting course. In brief, Evreinov's monodrama is the presentation of the point of view of a given individual on the level of his conscious and organizing intelligence.

By 1912, then, the second important direction of modern drama had been established, a direction which, since it deals with the rendering of inner truth, may be called pan-psychic. Much of the significant drama after 1912 is that drama which deals with the exploitation of the first person subjective point of view. Indeed, there was a veritable flood of experimentation with solutions to the new structural issue. In Germany there was the work of Kaiser, Toller, and the expressionists; in Italy, Pirandello and the writers of the grotesque theater; in France, the surrealists and Giraudoux; and in America, there were O'Neill, Rice, and even Kaufman and Connelly. Some of the more striking solutions to the problem of point of view included Pirandello's "theater in the theater" form, which presented various points of view of a single untold story; O'Neill's "simultaneous method," which blended a welter of conflicting viewpoints through the use of the once abhorred conventions of the aside and the soliloquy; and Giraudoux's presentation of a fairy tale through the point of view of the central character of the fantasy. Some of these solutions, like Giraudoux's *Madwoman of Chaillot,* have been simple. Some, like *Strange Interlude,* have been much too involved and subtle. All have been interesting.

A study of considerable length would be required to investigate adequately the scope and importance of pan-psychic experimentation with first person point of view, but we might pause here long enough to examine briefly one of the less complex but nonetheless interesting examples of the modern dramatist's exploitation of the new convention. The play is Kaiser's *From Morn to Midnight,* a work whose burden is the tragic plight of the modern individual ego. According to Kaiser, man is born perfect, but unhappily he is born into a malevolent social system which attempts to destroy his innate perfection. Thus, the individual is constantly at war with society, though most people are unaware of this conflict. At rare intervals, however, there appears an individual who gains insight into the nature of the struggle of which he is the protagonist. When this occurs, we have the Kaiserian New Man, a man who has an individ- ualized as opposed to a universalized point of view.[11] In order to protect his unique vision, the New Man may take, as does the Cashier in *From Morn to Midnight,* the impossible course of roman- tic escape. But flee as he might, society's force is overwhelming; and the New Man is doomed from the beginning to the tragic sur- render of his point of view to that of the group. *From Morn to Midnight* is a demonstration of this conflict and of its ultimate tragic end.

The play is divided into seven scenes whose only relationship to one another rests on the unity of central character and theme. The first two scenes introduce the Cashier and his antagonist society, and they deal with the creation of the Cashier as a New Man. They are, therefore, approached from the third person objective viewpoint. However, once the Cashier realizes that by his act of theft he has become an individual at war with the group, Kaiser underscores his new awareness by abruptly shifting in scene 3 to the first person subjective point of view. Thereafter, scenes 4, 5, and 6 present the Cashier's hopeless struggle with society; and thus they shift back and forth from third to first person point of view. Scene 4, for instance, although presented objectively, reflects in its quality the mood of the Cashier's soul; and the scene contains one speech by the Cashier which can only be described as a pure outpouring of his stream of consciousness. The following fragment of the speech is an example: "Parlour with table and hanging lamp, window with geraniums. Piano, music stool. Hearth—home fires burning. Kitchen—daily bread. Chops for supper."

In scene 5 Kaiser strikes a neat balance between the point of view of the Cashier and the more universal viewpoint of society as represented by the officials at the bicycle races. While the officials have eyes only for the races, the Cashier, in contrast, sees only the cheering crowd, which to him symbolizes the irrepressible flood of man's sacred and primal energy. Scene 6, on the other hand, shifts the emphasis in the direction of the Cashier's viewpoint, not because he is winning his battle with society, but because he is losing it. Since the Cashier's individuation has eroded beyond the point at which it offers a complementary contrast with society, Kaiser must place additional emphasis on the Cashier's point of view in order to bring into relief the few points of difference that remain. What is true of scene 6 is even more true of scene 7. The Cashier's unique outlook, which was in scenes 3, 4, and 5 a difference in kind from that of society, has by scene 7 become only a matter of a slight and ever diminishing difference in degree. Thus, in order to give adequate attention to the last stages of his surrender to the group, Kaiser projects the Salvation Army Hall scene entirely through the viewpoint of the Cashier. It is one of the most powerful scenes in modern dramatic literature and a brilliant example of the presentation of the first person subjective within the dramatic illusion. As the Cashier listens to sinners confess to crimes that are similar to his own, his will to resist weakens; and he ultimately abandons his private vision in favor of that of the group.

Among the many devices which Kaiser utilizes to reveal the Cashier's viewpoint, perhaps the most impressive is the playwright's handling of the crowd in scene 7. At the beginning of the scene, the crowd is highly individualized; but as the Cashier becomes more and more the victim of social erosion, as he returns once more to a sense of unity with the group, the crowd itself becomes gradually more unified. Finally, as the Cashier surrenders entirely and reunites himself with society, the crowd leaps to its feet to act as one great universal human machine.

After that point in scene 7 at which the Cashier surrenders, the scene quickly returns to the objectivity of third person. The Cashier bows to the inevitable and commits suicide; and the play closes on the flat, impersonal comment of the policeman: "There must be a short circuit in the main."

From Morn to Midnight is but one of many fine studies in point of view, studies which range from Ibsen's *Hedda Gabler* to Anouilh's *Waltz of the Toreadors*. They are not, by any means, all identical to the Kaiserian study, for each playwright used the convention in the manner best suited to state his own philosophy and aims. However, all reflect the modern playwright's concern with the first person point of view as the device best suited to the expression of the modern relativist's subjective creed. Moreover, so important is point of view in the history of modern drama that we may with some assurance say that it is the primary structural issue of all post-Ibsenian drama.

DONALD G. SCHUELER

SOME COMMENTS ON THE STRUCTURE OF JOHN GOWER'S *CONFESSIO AMANTIS*

EVERYONE who is at all familiar with John Gower's *Confessio Amantis* is aware that the title is exact: the poem is a lover's confession, confided to a confessor, Genius, who is supposed to be priest of Love. In keeping with this subject, all but one of the books[1] have as their central theme a particular sin against love; and all of these sins have various subdivisions, each of which the Confessor discusses and illustrates with at least one tale.

In the first three books of the poem, the method of subdividing the vices follows a clear-cut, rather geometric pattern. Pride, Envy, and Wrath, in that order, are the capital sins which Gower deals with; and each of these sins is defined in terms of five variations on it. Pride, for example, is presented by the Confessor in terms of Hypocrisy, Inobedience, Presumption, Avantance, and Vainglory.

This initial structural pattern in the *Confessio Amantis* of five-part subdivisions was beyond a doubt borrowed by Gower from his own earlier work, the *Mirour de l'Omme*. In a sizeable section of that poem he had presented the Seven Deadly Sins in their Christian context and had employed the same five variations of each sin which we find in the first books of the English poem. Moreover, the particular subdivisions used in the *Confessio Amantis* correspond exactly to those used in the *Mirour;* indeed, the structural parallels are so close that G. C. Macaulay, working from the *Confessio,* used this structural relationship as evidence in establishing that the redis-covered French poem was in fact Gower's.[2]

Yet in the *Confessio Amantis,* unlike the *Mirour,* Gower soon abandoned the five-part divisioning of sins with which he had begun. In the Fourth Book, he produced seven variations on the sin of Sloth. Besides this, the poet discarded the habit of allowing one or two, or at most, three tales to suffice as exempla of each variation. Under the subheading of Idleness, there are seven stories and anecdotes. Furthermore, some of these subdivisions and a very considerable number of the tales and digressions have only the thinnest con-nection, or none at all, with the theme of love. They are followed by discussions of alchemy, philosopher's stones, and language. In the Fifth and Sixth Books, the method of subdividing sins becomes even more variable, as do the number of exempla and the length of the digressions. And in the Seventh Book, Gower has even given up the idea of using a sin against love as the theme of that section; the whole book may be counted as a digression from the Lover's shrift.

In other words, by the time Gower had written a third of his poem he had begun to discard the neat system of departmentalization which he had obviously envisioned for the *Confessio* when he started it; and in the remaining books he never returned to it.

The questions which we must now ask ourselves, and which this paper will attempt to answer, are, first, why Gower gave up the "geometric" organization of the *Confessio Amantis* and, second, whether the later books of the poem are as structurally formless as the above description of them would seem to indicate.[3]

One answer to the first question is obvious: Gower abandoned the pattern which he had used in the *Mirour de l'Omme* because the sins which he had dealt with in that exclusively didactic work could not always apply to a discussion of love. But this could not have been his main reason. As a matter of fact, some of the subdivisions in the *Mirour* which he did not use in the *Confessio Amantis* might have been more appropriate than those he did use. For example, Superfluity and Prodigality could have been more appropriate as daughters of Love-Gluttony than his unhappy choice of Drunkenness (for which he mentions Tristan as an example); and under the head-ing of Lust (a sin which, except for the subdivision of Incest, he virtually ignores in his Eighth Book) he might have easily used all of the other four variations that are dealt with in the *Mirour.*

The main reason why Gower departed from this geometric kind of pattern was that he had discovered there was no need for it; the structure of his poem did not have to depend on so mechanical a device and would have been actually weakened by it. In the *Mirour de l'Omme,* Gower had been delivering a very long monologue, a poetic sermon, or, at any rate, a sermon in poetry; the tidy arrangement of information under departmental headings was useful in the same way that such arrangements still help to organize exceptionally long office memoranda. But in the *Confessio Amantis,* Gower was presenting a colloquy which required a method he had never used before, one which would take its rules from life rather than any textbook ideas of structure. For if the structural unity of a public monologue, that is, a lecture or a sermon, depends on the thematic continuity of the subject matter that is presented (which is the standard by which the *Mirour* should be judged and by which, incidentally, it succeeds more than most medieval didactic works), a dialogue, if it is to be worthy of the name, must depend for its structural integrity on the naturalness, not the formality, with which it flows along. A didactic monologue, such as the *Mirour,* may permissibly sound rehearsed; but the supposedly spontaneous confession of a Lover to a priest of Love cannot. It is a moot point whether Gower suspected that the departmentalization he had begun using in the English poem was actually giving his dialogue a "rehearsed" tone; what does seem certain is that he soon realized that the structure of his work depended, not on this geometric approach, but on whatever naturalness he was able to inject into the conversation and the characters of his two speakers. We must evaluate the architectonics of the *Confessio Amantis* on this basis. And on this basis, the poem succeeds more than has generally been acknowledged.

All things considered, the conversation that takes place between the Lover and the Confessor is in many ways a remarkably natural one. One should keep in mind the essentially static situation in which the action, such as it is, unfolds. There is no opportunity to observe either the Lover or Genius in the process of reacting to a variety of situations. Except for the beginning and end of the poem, they remain fixed, simply talking to each other, like characters in a Beckett play. Furthermore, both exist at least partially on an allegorical level, and their setting is the conventional one of the medieval dream vision.[4] Yet despite this burden of external unreality, neither the Lover nor the Confessor is a stock characterization, a mere puppet reciting Gower's ideas. The portrait of the Lover especially, is one of the most noteworthy and beguiling aspects of the poem. Almost all of the many passages in which he describes his thwarted affection for his lady are marked by an authenticity of feeling that still retains great charm. He is no Tristan, no Lancelot, no Troilus, but an aging, confused, and troubled fellow who has been caught up in a powerful emotion with which he knows not what to do. When the Confessor tells him he must be a gallant knight, traveling across the sea and fighting the heathens if he is to be worthy of his lady, the answer that he gives had never been heard before in all the pages of courtly literature:

> For this I telle you in schrifte,
> That me were levere hir love winne
> Than Kaire and al that is ther inne:
> And forto slen the hethen alle,
> I not what good ther mihte falle,
> So mochel blod thogh ther be schad.
> This finde I writen, hou Crist bad
> That noman other scholde sle.
> What scholde I winne over the Se,
> If I mi ladi loste at hom?
>   (IV, 1656–65)

All his comments are like that—direct, and movingly honest in a way that the usual courtly protestations of love almost never are.

As for the Confessor, although he remains an allegorical type, he is no mere mouthpiece for the objective knowledge he sets forth. Objective he is, because, as the Lover remarks, he is not emotionally engaged in the problems at hand. He is, in fact, the archetype of the garrulous but wise pedant. The Lover is almost always plaintive and to the point in his admissions and denials of sins against love, and in his remarks he reveals himself. The Confessor is invariably pontific and digressive, willing to keep his humble listener waiting while he displays his erudition for the benefit of the unseen audience that, in literature and life, always seems to accompany such figures. Behind every "Mi Sonne," with which Genius responds to the Lover's querulous questions and answers, one can hear an almost audible "Tut, tut."

Within this framework, the dialogue moves with a definite smooth-

ness. The Lover, helpless to help himself, is humbly dependent on
the Confessor; and until the very end he not only puts up with the
verbosity of his mentor, but encourages it by setting up the Confessor's responses:

> . . . and over this
> Of pride if ther oght elles is,
> Wherof that I me schryve schal,
> What thing it is in special,
> Mi fader, axeth, I you preie.
> Now lest, my Sone, and I schal seie. . . .
> (I, 1871–76)
>
> . . .
>
> Min herte is yit and evere was,
> As thogh the world scholde al tobrake,
> So ferful, that I dar noght speke
> Of what pourpos that I have nome,
> Whan I toward mi ladi come,
> But let it passe and overgo.
> Mi Sone, do nomore so. . . .
> (IV, 358–64)

This conversational give-and-take, although it hardly allows for the
kind of naturalness of language that is used in the *Canterbury Tales*,
is at least equally far removed from both the textbook question-and-
answer technique of the didacticists and the disputations of the
English debate-poems.

Furthermore, as the dialogue begins to break away from the rigid
departmentalization of sins against love with which it had begun,
the Confessor is able to discourse on an increasingly ethical, rather
than courtly, level without, however, transcending the general field
of secular knowledge. Digression, after all, was to be expected
both in the course of ordinary speech and in the pedantic character
of Genius. He becomes ambitious enough to be the spokesman for
the whole natural universe—this, without usually contradicting his
more limited representation of romantic love. For to Gower, love
was an aspect of the law of God.[5] Indeed, from the very earliest
pages he had freely mixed stories relating to sins against love with
stories that related the same sins to their generalized meanings as
sins against self, against mankind, and against God. Thus, for
example, under the single subdivision of Pride called Surquidry or
Presumption, we find the brief anecdote about Capaneus, who

neglects his religion and is struck down by God (I, 1977–2009); the tale of Narcissus, whose self-love brings him to his death (I, 2254–2366); and the story of the trumpet of death which blows for a king's brother, who is too prone to judge the weaknesses of his fellow man instead of his own (I, 2010–2253). Love is involved in each of these situations as either a sin or a virtue: self-love, love of man, love of God—but there is not a single story about Presumption that involves a romantic situation.

It is as early as these first lines, too, that the Confessor begins to speak for the natural law. The story of Narcissus serves as a fair example: after the young man has died for love of his own reflection, Gower describes his burial with some excellent lines and then draws his own moral from one of its poignant details:

> And thanne out of his sepulture
> Ther sprong anon par aventure
> Of floures such a wonder syhte,
> That men ensample take myhte
> Upon the dedes whiche he dede,
> As tho was sene in thilke stede;
> *For in the wynter freysshe and faire*
> *The floures ben, which is contraire*
> *To kynde, and so was the folie*
> *Which fell of his Surquiderie.*
>
> (I, 2343–52; [italics mine])

Genius consistently supports the natural law, everything that is "bei weie of kynde," and opposes what is "contraire to kynde." But Gower had to work out as he went along the means of giving his larger conception of Genius a freer rein. How free that meant becomes clear as the poem progresses. The Confessor not only contradicts the laws of courtly love when they contradict the law of nature, but, in the Fifth book, after failing to bypass a discussion of Venus, he also admits, when pressed by the Lover, that she is by no means omnipotent or even virtuous (1374–1443). The Confessor's attempt here to extricate himself from the narrower role of priest of Love is not a fortunate device on Gower's part; it is the one point in the poem when Genius' dual meaning becomes noticeably dichotomized. It does, however, indicate that Gower was becoming more and more aware of the possibilities of the figure. In general, Gower is more adept in his handling of these larger possibilities; he lets the reader draw his own conclusions from what Genius says, not about himself, but about the world around him. The technique is in this case analogous to the one which Gower uses to point up the Lover's age; it is simply a fact which is left to reveal itself. In the course of using this method, Gower actually brings the entire mechanism of the Lover's shrift to a halt. At the conclusion of the Sixth Book, the reader learns that there will be a hiatus in the confession. The Lover himself asks for a respite in order to learn how Alexander the Great was taught by Aristotle. The Confessor, characteristically, is only too pleased to oblige. After a modest disclaimer that, as priest of Venus, he knows nothing of such lofty matters, he embarks on the variety of subjects which comprise the Seventh Book. It should be mentioned that from the point of view of a purely geometric evaluation, this long digression is the worst of Gower's structural blunders. The poem is supposed to be a lover's confession; and the confession, with its logical use of divisions of sins and sub-sins, should constitute its structure. But this objection is more theoretical than factual. Normal conversation is not conducive to balance; it lends itself to digressions. If one reads the *Confessio Amantis* from beginning to end, one is liable to discover that the digressions seem to be the Confessor's, not Gower's. They halt the confession, but not the dialogue.

As a rule, the so-called digressions obtrude no more on the course of the conversation—and again, let me emphasize the distinction between "conversation" and "confession"—than do the innumerable stories which comprise most of the lines of the *Confessio Amantis*. And, like the digressions, these stories fit with a remarkable smoothness into the mainstream of dialogue. It is worth noting that, although the Confessor may be long-winded and discursive, in keeping with the sort of fellow he is, the characters in his tales never are. For Gower was a master of the action type of story. He left out nothing essential to his narratives, but he delivered them with an economy that left little room for ornamental descriptions and asides. They are spare and fast-paced in a way that usually works to their advantage. Much more than this could be said of Gower's storytelling art; but in our consideration of his poem's structure, we have only one point to make: the tales in the *Confessio Amantis* are rarely drawn-out, and before we know it we are back again with the Confessor and the Lover.

There is still another reason why the dialogue progresses with a minimum of artificiality: Gower's technical skill within the limits of the octosyllabic couplet has never been surpassed. A discussion of this facet of the poet's achievement, like that of his storytelling, belongs properly to another paper.[6] Here it is enough to briefly point out two facets of this achievement. One is the "perfectly simple and natural" way[7] in which Gower's sentences flow from line to line, emulating the normal rhythms of human speech and rarely falling into the jingling gait which is the chief danger of the meter he chose to use. The other concerns the distinctive difference that exists between the plaintive, hurried measure of the Lover's voice and the deeper, slower voice of Genius. It is chiefly a cumulative effect, but a passage may suggest it. The Confessor is expostulating in slow, balanced sentences against the vice of slander:

> And in this wise now a day
> In loves Court a man mai hiere
> Fulofte pleigne of this matiere,
> That many envious tale is stered,
> Wher that it mai noght ben ansuered;
> Bot yit fulofte it is believed,
> And many a worthi love is grieved
> Thurgh bacbitinge of fals Envie.
>   If thou have mad such janglerie
> In loves Court, mi Sone, er this,
> Schrif thee therof.
>
>   (II, 444–54)

To which the Lover replies with a quick admission, an equally sudden rhetorical question, and the headlong torrent of words in which, while admitting his guilt, he seeks to justify it:

>   Mi fader, yis:
> Bot wite ye how? noght openly,
> Bot otherwhile prively,
> Whan I my diere ladi mete,
> And thenke how that I am noght mete
> Unto hire hihe worthinesse,
> And ek I se the besinesse
> Of al this yonge lusty route,
> Which alday pressen hire aboute,
> And ech of hem his time awaiteth,
> And ech of hem his tale affaiteth,
> Al to deceive an innocent,
> Which woll noght ben of here assent. . . .
>
>   (II, 454–66)

This counterpoint is a matter of style as well as of content; the differing tones result not only from what is said but from the way it is said.

The elements in the *Confessio Amantis* which I have discussed above all contribute to the relative naturalness of that dialogue which comprises almost all the poem. And, as I have tried to indicate, the poem depends solely on the continuity of this dialogue for its organic structure—not on the geometric system of divisions of sins with which Gower began the *Confessio.* Since the conversational element is also introduced in the First Book, Gower can not be accused of substituting one structural technique for another in the middle of his work. However, he seems to have sensed that the continuing use of a rigid system of divisions and subdivisions of sins would eventually force the reader into an awareness of that contrived device and thus destroy the illusion of naturalness which he had created in the poem's dialogue. The technique of the confessional was still the useful excuse for innumerable tales, and the theme of aged love was still the means of reaching the poem's central moral— that all roads must in time lead to God. Gower had come to depend on the colloquy itself, not as a confession only, but as a wide-ranging discussion between a protagonist, who is man in his age, and that Genius who is the spirit not only of the law of love, but of all those natural laws which admonish and instruct man in the knowledge of his Creator.

Certainly this conversation is a "literary" device; and its purpose, aside from the conclusion, is plain enough: it allows for the maximum of entertainment and lore at which the poet aimed. However, hampered as he is by this heavy freight, Gower handles the dialogue very well. The proof of it is twofold: the Lover, and even the Confessor, become progressively better realized as the poem unfolds, and not once during its long course does the reader lose the sense of the continuity of their talk. This achievement has been, without exception, minimized by Gower's critics; yet no other Middle English writer of allegory, much less didactic allegory, could claim to have done as much in a work of comparable length. Form, or structure, was rarely a strong point of medieval writers, particularly when they departed from the technique of straightforward chronological narrative. In this company, Gower's poem is exceptional in terms of its sense of continuity, the more so in that it presents a static situation which in the hands of a Lydgate or a Jean de Meun would have become a series of disjointed tirades leading nowhere. Even *Piers the Plowman*, the only other long allegorical poem of any significance in Middle English, is a structural morass compared to the *Confessio Amantis*. This is not to say that the *Confessio Amantis* is a masterpiece of literary design in any absolute sense. But it does represent one of the very few major attempts made by fourteenth century English writers to transcend the stylized and often shapeless molds in which literature had been cast for centuries.

RAEBURN MILLER

THE PERSONS OF MOONSHINE:
A *Midsummer Night's Dream*
and the "Disfigurement" of Realities

Two worlds share the stage of A *Midsummer Night's Dream,* the wood and the city. The values they encompass are their usual ones: the wood—the natural, the primitive, the unknown, the inward; the city—the man-made, the civilized, the conscious, the outward. More than a contrast between rational and irrational or familiar and un- expected, the drama investigates a full range of relationships between fantasy and reality. Ultimately it is, indeed, a study of dream. The three sets of characters who find adventure in the wood reveal three varieties of fantasy. The lovers show the effect of un- reality on the private, average man; the clowns show its effect in the more public realm of art; and the fairies, for whom the wood is home, present fantasy completely disengaged from reality, the pure images of the dream state.

If the real world is, alas, subject to change and decay, the unreal world of the *Dream* suffers even more startlingly from such dis- tresses, and the methods by which it undergoes these losses are primarily what distinguish fantasy from the real during the play. In the wood—in woods—constancy rides on whim; four days pass in one night; the Queen Moon is only haply on her throne; and, most important, forms that in the city appeared substantial transform and reform suddenly, irrationally, capriciously; nothing is what it seems nor seems the same for long. It is through undergoing such experiences, as well as through their misconceptions of the experiences and of themselves, that the three sets of characters make clear this life within dream and illustrate their nature, their interrelation, and finally the resolution of their confusions in their return to the surer patterns of the city, the rational world.

The lovers begin the demonstration, revealing the impact of ir-rationality not on society as a whole nor in any unusual dimension, but on the individual man at the most striking—and most common—level. If the heroines differ from each other only in height,[1] they differ from us not at all; the very typicality of the four lovers rein-forces our sense of the kind of unreality they embody. Throughout the play their infidelities are, thanks to the fairies, the most intricate and mindless of the wood's confusions; but even when they are free from the influence of the magic flower, their moments of ac-curate perception are few. No world could be less substantial than that of these lovers, whose vagaries are only accelerated, not induced, by magic. Before the play's action begins, Demetrius has already shifted his affections arbitrarily from Helena to Hermia, and before the first scene is complete, Helena has decided to betray the confidence of her close friend. "Reason and love," as Bottom tells us in Act III, "keep little company together." Even in this first scene, love and young lovers are talked of as unreliable, not only by Egeus, who, after all, has a case to plead, but also by Theseus and the lovers themselves. Demetrius has been "spotted and inconstant"; Hermia, a "form in wax," is instructed to fit her "fancies" to her father's will; and Lysander presents a catalogue of ways true love has failed to run a smooth course, describing it finally as,

> . . . momentany as a sound,
> Swift as a shadow, short as any dream,
> Brief as the lightning in the collied night,
> That, in a spleen, unfolds both heaven and earth,
> And ere a man hath power to say "Behold!"
> The jaws of darkness do devour it up:
> So quick bright things come to confusion.
>   (I.i. 142–48)

The "graces" of her love have, for Hermia, "turned a heaven unto a hell," and Helena declares,

Things base and vile, holding no quantity,
Love can transpose to form and dignity.
Love looks not with the eyes, but with the mind;
And therefore is winged Cupid painted blind.
(I.i. 232–35)

In the wood, then, these inconstancies are magnified and exaggerated
by their setting, by their sudden freedom from rational restraint, so
that we see how much their true nature owes to the garblings of
fantasy.

If the lovers show unreality at work on a personal level, the
clowns—I had almost said *poets*—embody fantasy of another variety,
a more public and social adaptation of what is seen "not with the
eyes but with the mind." They are indeed "makers"—a carpenter, a
joiner, a weaver, a bellows-mender, a tinker, a tailor—but also in a
grander sense we watch them engaged in higher artistry, the pursuit
of aesthetic creation, the exercise of imagination not for personal but
for public gratification. Some of the confusions they labor with arise
from sweet ignorance, and their major encounter with the unreal—
Bottom's metamorphosis—is due to Puck's mischief. But even in
their first scene (I. ii.) they betray their subjection to illusion. They
are, after all, meeting to receive their roles in a play, to learn how
they are to transform themselves into what they are not; and "the
best in this kind are but shadows," as Theseus later reminds us. Yet
beyond the artificiality of the endeavor itself, the parts are ludicrous-
ly unsuited to the performers. That Flute, with beard coming or no,
should play Thisby is only slightly less fantastic than that Bottom
should undertake his condoling lover, and no mask can cover their
deficiencies. Bottom compounds his failure to see himself as he is by
imagining that he is qualified to assume all parts, that he even would
be able to act all at once. The complexities of his confusions are
indeed marvelous: if he may only be allowed to play the lion, he
assures us that the ladies will not mistake him for the real thing, for
he "will roar you as gently as any sucking dove." Once more, the
night's adventures in the wood isolate these contradictions for our
closer inspection and fuller understanding.

Still the lovers, however misguided, are men and act on mortal
presumptions; the clowns execute their daily crafts, we assume, with
a practicality that balances the folly of their higher calling. It is only
with the fairy court that we reach fantasy disembodied, the life of

unreality impeded by neither flesh nor conscience. Oberon is
"king of shadows" (III.ii. 347), the spirits of his court no more substantial than the moonlight by which they meet. Moreover, they
can transform themselves into various likenesses at will: in first
identifying himself, Puck describes his pleasure at playing a "filly
foal" and a "roasted crab," and later he proposes that

> Sometime a horse I'll be, sometime a hound,
> A hog, a headless bear, sometime a fire;
> And neigh, and bark, and grunt, and roar, and burn,
> Like horse, hound, hog, bear, fire, at every turn.
>   (III.i. 103–106)

Unreal themselves, their power lies in confounding the reality of
others, disrupting expected consequences, and changing truth to
dream. The results vary from cream that will not churn and stools
that topple wise aunts to changeling children and disastrous
weather; even the seasons reverse their ordered procession:

>   The spring, the summer,
> The chiding autumn, angry winter change
> Their wonted liveries, and the mazed world,
> By their increase, now knows not which is which.
>   (II.i. 111–14)

The extravagance of their transformations manifests the pure and
uncontrolled experience of fantasy which they serve to reveal.

The lovers, the clowns, and the fairies, then, present personal,
artistic, and wholly dreamlike imaginative worlds; but their useful-
ness for such representations makes them commonplace enough:
all lovers are deceived, all actors mimic, all fairies, I believe, indulge
at night in pranks. It is not the three groups in themselves that
interest us but rather their interaction; by showing the effects of one
kind of fantasy upon another, Shakespeare reveals both the nature of
the imagination and something of its proper uses. Of the interactions, the one most crucial to the plot is that between the lovers
and the fairies. We notice first that it is a one-way relationship: the
fairies act, but the lovers are merely acted upon and remain unaware
of the magic influences. Moreover, the interventions, whether deliberate or accidental, result only in exaggerating the distortions
already present; the object of love is made to change, but otherwise

the lover remains himself. If we are right in calling the fairies pure imagination, or, more timidly, the images of the unconscious mind, then fantasy as it reveals itself in daily life, the play suggests, is seldom recognized for what it is, however extensive. We pretend our most fanciful perceptions are just, acting on them as if they were rational and considered. And the influence, though powerful, is still partial, since it alters our actions rather than our natures. The result may be good, as eventually for Demetrius and Helena, or bad, as it threatens to be for Lysander and Hermia; but in either case the private life has been steered less by will than by caprice, by unreality.

The relations between the clowns and the fairies, however, are more complicated, for here we find a mutual influence. Bottom is translated, but Titania also undergoes a magic spell and wakes from her love for the ass to find her own world changed, herself and Oberon "new in amity." And the experience has been no less significant for Bottom. Beyond the considerable reward of enjoying the favors of a figure so fine as Titania, he has, if briefly, been transported to a higher order of existence. The world he shares with the Queen is one which reconciles man, beast, and spirit in ease and love. It is surely no accident that he reports his inability to describe his dream in the words Paul applied to "the things that God hath prepared for them that love him" (I Cor. 2:9) nor that upon returning to himself his first thought is to have Peter Quince fix the dream in a song. Accepting Theobald's "after" for "at her," we may even be forgiven for finding double significance in his closing remark: "I will sing it in the latter end of a play, before the duke. Peradventure, to make it the more gracious, I shall sing it after death" (IV.i. 218 ff.). The artist's encounter with the imagination is more fruitful than the lover's It resolves conflicts and contradictions within the imagination itself and provides the artist at least with a work of art and possibly with an insight into an ultimate and better truth.

The lovers and the clowns never meet one another in the wood, but at the celebration in Act V they are brought together both physically as audience and performers and also more intimately through the material of the "most Lamentable Comedy." Indeed, it is in the city that all three groups of characters find their reconciliation. In the wood they have served to show us their fantasies unrestrained; in the city we see how the ordered way of life established by the mature and rational Theseus[2] incorporates fantasy meaningfully into a total system. Here the lovers, by participating with Theseus in that central ritual of civilized society, the marriage ceremony, resolve their confusions and establish a safe and lasting union. The poets achieve even more. In the court they too are safe at last to fulfill themselves in the performance of the play, an action found impossible in the incoherent wood. But more important, through their play itself they take the sentiments we have laughed at the lovers for treating seriously and by the artistic act transform those sentiments into a new reality, both more serious, and yet more laughable, than the old. Bottom has had his share in reconciling the fairy marriage. Now he and his fellows show how a tragic end to the course of true love may also, by being removed through art from the personal fancy to the social and public work of imagination, come to be lifted above the trivial. If they are unskillful in presenting their play, Shakespeare's point is only that much clearer; the activity of even the worst artist is redemptive, and Theseus is just in his commendation. Finally, the fairies reappear, and we find they too are changed by their arrival in Athens. Whereas in the wood they were mischievous and even, through their effect on the weather, destructive, here they are wholly benevolent, blessing the house and its marriages. Their powers to transform are now used to protect the future offspring from disfigurement. Even the pure phantoms of fancy, when operating in a stable social order, have their comforts and their joy.

Oberon, Lysander, and Peter Quince, then, are of imagination all compact. Perhaps Hippolyta is correct when she declares that the lovers' account of their night in the woods "more witnesseth than fancy's images"; at least it witnesses that much, and possibly her testimony is made suspect when she can exclaim later over Pyramus and Thisby, "This is the silliest stuff that ever I heard." It may be that by the time she finds herself actually pitying Pyramus (V.i. 288) she has come to realize how much fancy's images can "witness." Surely Theseus, though he may not believe "these fairy toys," has correctly identified the basis of the events (V.i. 2 ff.); and when he answers Hippolyta's objections to the play with, "The best in this kind are but shadows; and the worst are no worse, if imagination amend them," we see he has a true appreciation of the place of fantasy in human affairs, the place assigned it not merely by his remark but by the total action of this play. As Puck declares in his epilogue, this is a work "no more yielding but a dream"; yet here too Puck is mocking foolish mortals: it is precisely as a dream that the play yields most.

COOPER R. MACKIN

AURAL IMAGERY AS MILTONIC METAPHOR:
The Temptation Scenes of
Paradise Lost and *Paradise Regained*

DESPITE ONE of the most venerable commonplaces of Milton criticism
—that *Paradise Lost* is a visual poem—the crucial temptation scene is
pervaded by aural, not visual, imagery. The climax comes in Book
IX, when Eve eats the forbidden fruit:

> Earth felt the wound, and Nature from her seat
> Sighing through all her Works gave signs of woe,
> That all was lost.   (IX, 782–84)[1]

And later in the same book, when Adam eats,

> Nature gave a second groan,
> Skie lowr'd and muttering Thunder, som sad drops
> Wept at compleating of the mortal Sin
> Original.   (IX, 1001-1004)

I suggest that this aural imagery is a metaphor for the ultimate meaning of Satan's temptation and that it serves the same function in the
temptation scenes of *Paradise Regained*. Both Eve and Christ are
tempted to disrupt God's harmonious order.

   The interest in the concept of world harmony (*discordia concors*),
which was evident in the Middle Ages and the early Renaissance,
carried over to the later Renaissance and is central to an examination
of Milton's aural patterns. The definitive study of this concept is
Leo Spitzer's *Classical and Christian Ideas of World Harmony*.[2]

32

Professor Spitzer points out how, especially in music, there was in the Middle Ages a shift in form from monody to polyphony or harmony. The emphasis remained on an ultimate "oneness," but a oneness composed of many disparate parts and obtaining its beauty from the ability of its components to harmonize. This musical harmony was then seen as a metaphor for the harmonious unity of the world: "The idea of world harmony, in which music is seen as symbolizing the totality of the world, is an idea which was ever present to the mind of the Middle Ages"; an important corollary is that the "harmony of the cosmos, like that of music, is a gift of grace. . . . Since harmony and music can be conceived as one, we may . . . find the triad, grace-nature-harmony."[3] Professor Spitzer's comments might well have been made specifically about *Paradise Lost*. In the Miltonic cosmo-theology, harmony, a sign of grace, is a heavenly or Godlike attribute; disharmony, a sign of sin, is a chaotic or Satanic one. For Milton, this identification is constantly present. We read in Book VII of *Paradise Lost* that at the creation,

> Heav'n op'nd wide
> Her ever during Gates, Harmonious sound
> On golden Hinges moving, to let forth
> The King of Glorie in his powerful Word
> And Spirit coming to create new Worlds.
>   (VII, 205–209)

On the other hand, when Sin opens "Hell Gate" in Book II,

> on a sudden op'n flie
> With impetuous recoile and jarring sound
> Th' infernal dores, and on thir hinges grate
> Harsh Thunder, that the lowest bottom shook
> Of *Erebus*.   (II, 879–83)

This contrast between portal concord on the one hand and portal discord on the other is expressive of an aural pattern which recurs throughout the poem. Since the contrast exists, it is fitting that Satan's temptations be metaphorized as attempts to disrupt the harmonious order of nature, thereby hindering the extension of grace.

The aural imagery in the temptations is anticipated most notably by the discord characterizing the battle in heaven. That scene is set in Book V, where Raphael tells Adam about God's elevation of His son to the status of "Vice-gerency." The loyal angels celebrate their joy by the harmonious motions of *discordia concors,* and "in thir motions harmonie Divine / So smooths her charming tones, that Gods own ear / Listens delighted" (V, 625–27). Then all sleep ". . . save those who in thir course / Melodious Hymns about the sovran Throne / Alternate all night long: but not so wak'd / *Satan*" (V, 655–58). Satan is already in secret opposition to the divine harmony. As open opposition nears, the "loud / Ethereal Trumpet from on high gan blow" as a signal for the heavenly forces to move to the attack, "to the sound / Of instrumental Harmonie that breath'd / Heroic Ardor to advent'rous deeds" (VI, 64–66). When the battle begins—when Satan tries to destroy the divinely instituted order— "the shout / Of Battel now began, and rushing sound / Of onset ended soon each milder thought" (VI, 96–98). Discord rages until Messiah restores concord and the celestial army, composed of many disparate components, becomes united under him (VI, 777–82); as he drives Satan and his crew from heaven, "Hell heard th' unsufferable noise . . . confounded Chaos roar'd."

Finished with his narrative to Adam, Raphael refers to the battle as "the discord which befell," and specifically warns Adam against Satan, at the same time making explicit the vocality of the temptation:

> But list'n not to his Temptations, warne
> Thy weaker; let it profit thee to have heard
> By terrible Example the reward
> Of disobedience; firm they might have stood,
> Yet fell; remember, and fear to transgress.
> (VI, 908–12)

Satan is a force working against the will of God, and hence tending to disrupt the order of God's created universe. But he is also a dissembler, adept at blurring the distinction between appearance and reality, both for his own followers and during his temptations of Eve and Christ. Part of Eve's guilt lies in not being sufficiently cautious to detect this confusion; a good deal of Christ's power to resist Satan stems from his astuteness at perceiving and pointing out the distinction. At this level of interpretation, as at the other, Milton's metaphorical use of aural imagery is clear: Satan will conjure up what seems to be harmony and concord but what is in fact only discord, more or less effectually concealed.

This Satanic tactic is adumbrated in Book II of *Paradise Lost,* immediately after the great conclave in hell. Here there is first an ironic parody of the continuous choir of angels around the throne of God and especially of its acclaiming Messiah with loud Hosannas:

> Then of thir Session ended they bid cry
> With Trumpets regal sound the great result:
> Toward the four winds four speedy Cherubim
> Put to thir mouths the sounding Alchymie
> By Haralds voice explain'd: the hollow Abyss
> Heard farr and wide, and all the host of Hell
> With deafning shout, return'd them loud acclaim.
> (II, 514–20)

Then, as the devilish hosts disband to amuse themselves until Satan's return, there occurs what seems harmonious, plaintive, even gentle music and song:

> Others more milde,
> Retreated in a silent valley, sing
> With notes Angelical to many a Harp
> Thir own Heroic deeds and hapless fall
> By doom of Battel; and complain that Fate
> Free Vertue should enthrall to Force or Chance.
> Thir song was partial, but the harmony
> (What could it less when Spirits immortal sing?)
> Suspended Hell, and took with ravishment
> The thronging audience. In discourse more sweet
> (For Eloquence the Soul, Song charms the Sense,)
> Others apart sat on a Hill retir'd [.]
> (II, 546–57)[4]

There is even an ironic reference to *discordia concors*: though their song was partial (composed of many parts), it was harmonious. But Milton immediately reveals that what has seemed harmonious and genuine is actually false: "Vain wisdom all, and false Philosophie" (II, 565).

If, however, Satan's minions are able to dissemble harmony, the fiend himself is more involved in reality as he arrives at the gate of Hell and confronts his offspring Sin. Since she is a direct result of Satan's disobedient nature, she is surrounded by wild disorder and disharmony:

> . . . about her middle round
> A cry of Hell Hounds never ceasing bark'd
> With wide *Cerberean* mouths full loud, and rung
> A hideous Peal: yet, when they list, would creep,
> If aught disturb'd thir noyse, into her woomb,
> And kennel there, yet there still bark'd and howl'd
> Within unseen.   (II, 653–59)

The Son's words of creation will be an admonishment to harmony: "Silence, ye troubl'd waves, and thou Deep, peace, / Said then th' Omnific Word, your discord end" (VII, 216–17). But Satan must travel through the place where "eldest Night / And *Chaos*, Ancestors of Nature, hold / Eternal Anarchie, amidst the noise / Of endless warrs, and by confusion stand" (II, 894–97).

I have developed these ideational threads at such length because they form a necessary background for a clear understanding of the role played by aural imagery in and around the temptation scenes. In Book V of *Paradise Lost*, Eve tells Adam of her dream of the previous night, which had been prompted by Satan's whispering in her ear as she slept:

> . . . methought
> Close at mine ear one call'd me forth to walk
> With gentle voice, I thought it thine; it said,
> Why sleepst thou *Eve?* now is the pleasant time,
> The cool, the silent, save where silence yields
> To the night-warbling Bird, that now awake
> Tunes sweetest his love-labor'd song.
>   (V, 35–41)

Milton later makes clear (V, 67–81) that the temptation of the dream was for Eve to try to rise in the chain of being, thereby disrupting the natural order of divine harmony. Because Eve is still in the state of grace and can "hear" the harmony of nature, Satan's technique of confusing appearance and reality (the voice sounded like Adam's) centers in an appeal to the sense of hearing. An especially subtle device is the presence of a singing bird to suggest that no disruption or discord is imminent. By the seventeenth century, there had long been a tradition that singing birds are symbolic of harmony and order. In Professor Spitzer's words: "Once it became possible to present a particular being as attuning his soul to the music of the world—his voice being considered as one instrument more in the world concert of praise to God—there was nothing to prevent the acceptance of caroling birds as fellow-musicians."[5] The obvious implication is that caroling birds may be considered symbols of order since they are attuned to the celestial music. In an early exercise, Milton had written, "We may well believe that it is in order to tune their own notes in accord with that harmony of heaven to which they listen so intently, that the lark takes her flight up into the clouds at daybreak and the nightingale passes the lonely hours of night in song."[6]

The result of the episode in Book IV is that Satan is apprehended by Gabriel's patrol, but he has succeeded in preparing Eve for the actual temptation. In Book IX, as Eve goes about her work, "shee busied heard the sound / Of rusling Leaves, but minded not, as us'd / To such disport before her through the Field" (IX, 518–20). She ignores the sound, and soon Satan begins his temptation:

> . . . he glad
> Of her attention gaind, with Serpent Tongue
> Organic, or impulse of vocal Air,
> His fraudulent temptation thus began.
> (IX, 528–31)

Throughout the temptation, Milton's insistence on the serpent's unnatural power of speech indicates an ignored warning on Eve's part:

> Into the Heart of *Eve* his words made way,
> Though at the voice much marveling.
> . . . .
> Thee, Serpent, suttlest beast of all the field
> I knew, but not with human voice endu'd;
> Redouble then this miracle, and say,
> How cam'st thou speakable of mute[?]
> (IX, 550–51; 560–63)

As the temptation progresses, we are increasingly aware of the concept of Satan as orator, which has its beginnings in his first appearance in Book I and which is developed as he whispers into Eve's ear in Book IV.[7] Traditionally, the power of speech was equated with reason and thus formed the chief distinction between man and beast in the scale of existence; traditionally also, reason was equated with harmony and order. When the entire temptation scene is examined in the light of these traditions, its aural orientation is unsurprising: Satan, taking the form of a mute serpent, assumes the power of speech, and *discordia concors* is already broken. But through this very power (oratory), he is able to confuse appearance and reality to the extent that Eve not only ignores the natural disruption already present, but is persuaded, in the implicit interests of harmony ("reason"), to cause an even greater break: ". . . in her ears the sound / Yet rung of his perswasive words, impregn'd / With Reason, to her seeming, and with Truth" (IX, 736–38).[8] The steady intensification of aural imagery is climaxed, as we have seen, when Eve finally eats:

> Earth felt the wound, and Nature from her seat
> Sighing through all her Works gave signs of woe,
> That all was lost.
>
> (IX, 782–84)

And when Eve beseeches Adam "with bland words" to eat also, and he eats,

> Nature gave a second groan
> Skie lowr'd and muttering Thunder, som sad drops
> Wept at compleating of the mortal Sin
> Original.   (IX, 1001-1004)

All nature groans at the disruption of *discordia concors*: discordant sound symbolizes the total discord resulting from original sin.

This aural symbolism also pervades Christ's temptations in *Paradise Regained*. After he dreams of food in Book II,

> Thus wore out night, and now the Herald Lark
> Left his ground-nest, high towring to descry
> The morns approach, and greet her with his Song.
>   (II, 279–81)

The presence of the lark underlines Christ's harmony with God. Now Satan begins his temptation: as Christ climbs a hill, he "Only in a bottom saw a pleasant Grove, / With chaunt of tuneful Birds resounding loud" (II, 289–90). The birds are here also, but now Christ must pierce the veil between appearance and reality: a few lines later we read, "Natures own work it seem'd (Nature taught Art)," an indication that this valley has been conjured by Satan. He has placed birds here, as in Eve's dream, as a subtle implication of harmony. A similar technique occurs when Satan spreads his sumptuous banquet, for "all the while Harmonious Airs were heard / Of chiming strings, or charming pipes" (II, 362–63). If Christ succumbs to this spell of seeming harmony, Satan will be the victor. But Jesus immediately penetrates the guise: "Thy pompous Delicacies I contemn, / And count thy specious gifts no gifts but guiles" (II, 390–91). Thereupon, "Both Table and Provision vanish'd quite / With sound of Harpies wings, and Talons heard" (II, 402–403), a swift change from the guileful harmony of the temptation.[9]

Satan's oratory, which had served him so well with Eve, is powerless before the God-man. Christ points to this fact, at the same time emphasizing the vocality of Satan's temptations—not the visuality—after the prospect from the mountain:

> . . . in my ear
> [Thou hast] Vented much policy, and projects deep
> Of enemies, of aids, battels and leagues,
> Plausible to the world, to me worth naught.
> (III, 390–93)

Having failed in this, Satan tries another tack: his next temptation, to fear, comes during the storm and is permeated by discordant noise; but Christ, in perfect harmony with God, is unmoved:

> The Tempter watch'd, and soon with ugly dreams
> Disturb'd his sleep; and either Tropic now
> 'Gan thunder, and both ends of Heav'n, the Clouds
> From many a horrid rift abortive pour'd
> Fierce rain with lightning mixt, water with fire
> In ruine reconcil'd: nor slept the winds
> Within thir stony caves, but rush'd abroad
> From the four hinges of the world.
> . . . .
> Infernal Ghosts, and Hellish Furies, round
> Environ'd thee, some howl'd, some yell'd, some shriek'd,
> Some bent at thee thir fiery darts, while thou
> Sat'st unappall'd in calm and sinless peace.
> (IV, 408–25)[10]

Christ's successful resistance of the temptation leads to a reassertion of harmony, as symbolic of his continued and unmitigated unity with the father:

> [Morning] with her radiant finger still'd the roar
> Of thunder. . . .
> . . . .
>   . . . the birds
> Who all things now behold more fresh and green,
> After a night of storm so ruinous,
> Clear'd up their choicest notes in bush and spray
> To gratulate the sweet return of morn.
>   (IV, 428–38)

Finally, after Christ's terminal victory over Satan on the pinnacle of
the temple, ". . . Angelic Quires / Sung Heavenly Anthems of his
victory / Over temptation, and the Tempter proud" (IV, 593-95).
The triumph of Christ over Satan is the triumph of harmony over
discord, order over chaos, and it is expressed aurally. Even as
Satan has dared tempt the son of God with his voice, so will he be
punished by the son's voice:

>   . . . he all unarm'd
> Shall chase thee with the terror of his voice
> From thy Demoniac holds, possession foul,
> Thee and thy Legions, yelling they shall flye.
>   (IV, 626–29)

The three human figures in *Paradise Lost* and *Paradise Regained*
face their crucial tests in vocal contexts; it is only a fourth, however,
who can show us the structural justification for these contexts. He
has plummeted, with Satan and us, down into the "*Stygian* Pool";
he has been "Taught by the heav'nly Muse to venture down / The
dark descent, and up to reascend." But in the Invocation to Book
VII of *Paradise Lost*, these typical counters of the poem's spatial
structure are fused with the traditionally aural covenant of poet and
muse. Milton has carried us with him to the lowest depths, the most
exalted heights; but he in turn has been carried by a voice:

> Descend from Heav'n *Urania*, by that name
> If rightly thou art call'd, whose Voice divine
> Following, above th' *Olimpian* Hill I soare,
> Above the flight of *Pegasean* wing.
>   (VII, 1–4)

The poet, singing "More safe . . . with mortal voice," remains
"unchang'd / To hoarce or mute, though fall'n on evil dayes, /

... and evil tongues" because his inspiration is "Heav'nlie." Like the archetypal poet Orpheus, however, he is beset by discordant dangers:

> But drive farr off the barbarous dissonance
> Of *Bacchus* and his Revellers, the Race
> Of that wilde Rout that tore the *Thracian* Bard
> In *Rhodope*, where Woods and Rocks had Eares
> To rapture, till the savage clamor dround
> Both Harp and Voice.
>
> (VII, 32–37)

Milton's consistent and persistent use of the mode of paradox[11] gives us the perspective we need to properly assess the aural imagery surrounding the temptations in *Paradise Lost* and *Paradise Regained*. If darkness is Satan's ambience, still God is "Dark with excessive bright"; if Adam and Eve sin in the brightness of high noon, still the sin is "fortunate." If Satan can pervert the great symbol of man's reason to cause the fall, still Urania (who from eternity "didst play / In presence of th' Almightie Father") can transcend the fall with the same symbol, leading poet and reader, "Earthlie Guest[s]," into the "Heav'n of Heav'ns." Satan's nocturnal whispers into Eve's ear in Book IV must be balanced against the image in Book VII of Urania's nightly visitations.

In an early poem, "At a Solemn Musick," Milton had besought the celestial Sirens, symbol of harmony, to "Wed your divine sounds, and mixt power employ / Dead things with inbreath'd sense able to pierce," so that:

> ... we on Earth with undiscording voice
> May rightly answer that melodious noise;
> As once we did, till disproportion'd sin
> Jarr'd against natures chime, and with harsh din
> Broke the fair musick that all creatures made
> To their great Lord, whose love their motion sway'd
> In perfet Diapason, whilst they stood
> In first obedience, and their state of good.
> O may we soon again renew that Song,
> And keep in tune with Heav'n, till God ere long
> To his celestial consort us unite,
> To live with him, and sing in endles morn of light.

Before the fall, the great and beautiful idea of *discordia concors* was a reality, all the disparate components of nature uniting their voices in a harmonious hymn to God. Temptation, succumbed to, breaks union with God and mars this harmony; but through grace man may return to that prelapsarian harmony which existed after the creation. In the crucial scenes of *Paradise Lost* and *Paradise Regained,* as in "At a Solemn Musick," Milton's metaphor of sin as aural discord, grace as aural concord, seems inevitable.

SERAPHIA LEYDA

"LOVE'S RARE UNIVERSE":
Eros in Shelley's Poetry

ALTHOUGH it has become a critical cliché to state that love is an important concept and theme in the poetry of Shelley, few attempts have been made to deal with this aspect of Shelley's work through a direct appraisal of the poems. This paper examines Shelley's concept of eros as defined by its thematic and structural function in several of his love poems. My purpose is to allow Shelley the poet to speak through his poetry rather than to impose upon that poetry more of the heavy burdens of psychological, biographical, philosophical, or critical preconceptions which it has had to bear in the past. My only assumptions will be that the poetry of Shelley is good enough to merit such attention and great enough to survive such meddling.

In Shelley's poetry, erotic love is consistently characterized by sympathy and the "void." Sympathy has two faces in Shelley's poetry. With one face it looks upon all things and creatures in the universe and uncritically embraces them. With its other face, sympathy views all things and finds them alien. It focuses upon human kind and seldom sees a man or a woman who can respond to the feeling or return the understanding which it so urgently presses upon them. This situation leads to the experience of the "void" and, consequently, to the motif of solitude and possible destruction. The lover, for all his sympathy, can find no one to love.

43

This paradox does not arise from the doctrine of sympathy itself but from the character of the lover.

The Poet in *Alastor*, Prince Athanase, Lionel, the Maniac in *Julian and Maddalo*, and the lover in *Epipsychidion* all pass through, although some do not survive, what I shall call a crisis of sympathy. This crisis is a direct result of the character's psychological makeup and his experience of the void.[1] Lionel and the lover in *Epipsychidion* survive this experience; the *Alastor* poet dies; the Maniac in *Julian and Maddalo* goes mad; we can only guess what happens to Athanase. Eros appears to be destructive. The void cannot be filled or navigated. However, I hope to show that this apparent destructiveness of eros is not real or, at least, that Shelley did not view erotic love as necessarily destructive. Shelley's concept of eros was a developing one although its final form was inherent in its beginnings.

Alastor introduces us to what will become a standard treatment of the romantic hero in Shelley's poetry. In the Wordsworthian manner, we are given a sketch of the Poet's infancy, childhood, and youth. The ministry of beauty and of fear which fostered the poet of *The Prelude* are replaced here by "solemn vision, and bright silver dream," preparing us for the more mystical, idealized figure of Shelley's poet who leaves his "cold fireside and alienated home / To seek strange truths in undiscovered lands."[2] The idealistic level is reached quickly, and the reader moves easily into a world whose reality is emblematic and intellectual.

The wanderings of our vegetarian hero lead him through nature and ancient civilizations, until

> . . . meaning on his vacant mind
> Flashed like strong inspiration, and he saw
> The thrilling secrets of the birth of time.
>   (ll. 126–28, 18)

Up to this point of fulfillment the Poet has been alone. We have only seen him moving against a background of natural phenomena or ruined buildings. Although we are told earlier by the narrator of his effect on other human beings—

> Strangers have wept to hear his passionate notes,
> And virgins, as unknown he passed, have pined
> And wasted for fond love of his wild eyes.
>   (ll. 61–63, 16)

—we never see him in juxtaposition with his own kind until the appearance of the lovelorn Arab maiden. The Poet is evidently unconscious of his disastrous effect on her—"to her cold home / Wildered, and wan, and panting, she returned . . ." (ll. 138–39, 18)—for he wanders on without any sign of concern or regret. His solitude is unbroken even in the company of one who loves him.

In strong contrast to his indifference toward the Arab maiden is his immediate and deep response to the "veilèd maid" of his vision. The dream figure in its perfection casts a long shadow on the Arab maiden or any real woman the Poet may meet. This vision, in spite of veils and high poetic themes, is not all spirit and intellect.[3] The physical presence of the veiled maid is the most intoxicating aspect of her appearance and compels the Poet to a physical, erotic response. The high themes of her lofty discourse have an immediate physical effect on herself as well as on the Poet:

> . . . Soon the solemn mood
> Of her pure mind kindled through all her frame
> A permeating fire. . . .
> (ll. 161–63, 18)

This immediate translation of thought into emotion is characteristic of all Shelley's poetry and illustrates his belief in the intimate relationship between these two sides of human nature. When, in her agitation, she rises, the Poet

> . . . saw by the warm light of their own life
> Her glowing limbs beneath the sinuous veil
> Of woven wind, her outspread arms now bare,
> Her dark locks floating in the breath of night,
> Her beamy bending eyes, her parted lips
> Outstretched, and pale, and quivering eagerly.
> (ll. 175–80, 19)

Every detail emphasizes the erotic, the physical passion which the vision has "kindled" in herself. Her bare arms, her "parted lips/ . . . quivering eagerly," and particularly her "glowing limbs" visible beneath the "sinuous veil" are unmistakable in their intention. Indeed, the Poet's spontaneous reaction is understandable considering the provocation: "His strong heart sunk and sickened with ex-

cess / Of love" (ll. 181–82, 19). Together with the visionary, idealized qualities of the female-poet, exist the passionate, physical
demands of eros.

The vision dissolves, and the poem has only just begun; more than
five hundred lines follow in which we watch the disintegration of
the Poet. His actions are made more sympathetic than those of
Hippolytus, but his doom is no less certain:

> The spirit of sweet human love has sent
> A vision to the sleep of him who spurned
> Her choicest gifts. He eagerly pursues
> Beyond the realms of dream that fleeting shade;
> He overleaps the bounds. Alas! Alas![4]
>   (ll. 203–207, 19)

He cannot rid himself of the passion which is compared to a "fierce
fiend of a distempered dream" (l. 225, 20) and a "green serpent"
(l. 228, 20) which grasps an eagle in its folds. Earth is no longer a
beautiful and joyous place:

>   . . . His wan eyes
> Gaze on the empty scene as vacantly
> As ocean's moon looks on the moon in heaven.
>   (ll. 200–202, 19)

After his wanderings, he dies calmly and peacefully as the "great
moon" sinks behind the "jaggèd hills." In the careful analogy of his
dying with the setting of the moon, the narrator indicates the close
relationship of the Poet and Nature:

>   . . . the Poet's blood,
> That ever beat in mystic sympathy
> With nature's ebb and flow, grew feebler still. . . .
>   (ll. 651–53, 29)

The Poet's withdrawal disrupted his relationship with Nature but
could not destroy it. On the other hand, the change passion
wrought in the Poet did alter his tenuous relationship with other
human beings. Their reactions to him as an alien, fearful creature,
reinforce his isolation from his own kind; even

> . . . the infant would conceal
> His troubled visage in his mother's robe
> In terror at the glare of those wild eyes,
> To remember their strange light in many a dream
> Of after-times. . . .
>
> (ll. 262–66, 20–21)

Only the "youthful maidens, taught / By nature" still felt sympathy for him (ll. 266–271, 21). The Poet, in his alienation, remains oblivious to all these reactions. He has cut himself off from any meaningful relationship with other humans; and although he is the cause of sympathy in others, he does not extend sympathy.

In his preface to *Alastor*, Shelley notes, "The intellectual faculties, the imagination, the functions of sense, have their respective requisitions on the sympathy of corresponding powers in other human beings." Each of these three "powers" has its correspondent as shown in the following:

Conversant with speculations of the sublimest and the most perfect natures, the vision in which he embodies his own imaginations unites all of the wonderful, or wise, or beautiful, which the poet, the philosopher, or the lover could depicture (14).

If we arrange these triple series of threes into one three-fold grouping, we arrive at the following: intellectual faculties—philosopher— the wise; imagination—poet—the wonderful; functions of sense— lover—the beautiful. It becomes obvious that Shelley's heroes must possess intelligence, imagination, and sensation; they are philosopher-poet-lovers. The union of these superior qualities in one human being constitutes the superiority of each Shelleyan hero to the multitude of other men and women who may have only one, or none, or a bad combination of the three powers. Such natural superiority, not inherited titles or lands, produces nobility and elevated status in Shelley.

Eros, then, for such a man involves not only the sensuous aspects of man's nature but the intellectual and imaginative as well. The unity of these three "powers" does not diminish the importance of any one of them; rather such a unity raises each to its highest degree of perfection. In *Alastor*, "The Poet is represented as uniting these requisitions, and attaching them to a single image. He seeks in vain for a prototype of his conception" (15). Such unity and such perfection are not to be found on earth.

But the Poet's idealistic fantasy is not entirely baseless. Shelley tells us that his mind "is at length suddenly awakened and thirsts for intercourse with an intelligence similar to itself. He images to himself the Being whom he loves" (14). The Poet has used his own mind, imagination, and senses as measurements and guidelines for his vision. If he exists, why can not another being like himself exist? This is not unreasonable; it is only impossible, for in taking the mirror image of himself and changing its sex, he also removes any flaws or wavy lines of human limitation or imperfection. The result is not a photographic reproduction but a highly idealistic work of art. And we must not forget that this vision is sent him by the "spirit of sweet human love" because he spurned her choicest gifts. The unattainable perfection of his vision is not entirely his own doing. He is a victim as well as the perpetrator of his veiled lady.[5]

His obsession leads to the unpardonable romantic sin, lack of sympathy for and isolation from other human beings. Yet the poem's treatment of the Poet is not harsh; the narrator does not prevent the inevitable punishment, but he throws a tragic and sympathetic color over the transgressor.[6] The ambiguity of the passion—

> The meeting boughs and implicated leaves
> Wove twilight o'er the Poet's path, as led
> *By love, or dream, or god, or mightier Death,*
> He sought in Nature's dearest haunt, some bank,
> Her cradle, and his sepulchre. . . .
> (ll. 426–30, 24, [italics mine])

—perhaps arises from the intermixture of virtue, the search for love, with vice, the failure of sympathy. In this context, the destructive force of the passion does not wholly stem from the compulsion of eros.

The same ambiguity clings to the roles of death and solitude and their relationship to eros. The three could be ranged in a causal chain: solitude rouses eros; eros causes death; however, this relationship hardly stands up under closer scrutiny. The Poet's solitude in the first part of the poem is not presented as evil. Although it does eventually lead to his vision and consequently his downfall, the solitude appears almost necessary for his "education." Nor is eros fatal to all; the Arab maiden survives, though we may speculate about her future unhappiness. Death itself is finally calm and peace after the ravages of his quest. So we must conclude that none of these three is in itself bad. It is the unfortunate combination of solitude, eros, and death together with the unusual character of the Poet which precipitate the tragedy.

In his preface to *Alastor*, Shelley comments on the hero: "The Poet's self-centred seclusion was avenged by the furies of an irresistible passion pursuing him to speedy ruin" (15). That "irresistible passion" is erotic, but it is not eros. We may tentatively draw a distinction between erotic passion and eros. The erotic passion scourges the Poet toward death when it cannot find its proper object. Thus the inability to find such an object creates erotic passion closely related to death.[7] If and when the proper object were found, the erotic passion would be metamorphosed into eros—a relationship of love between two human beings.

Unlike the Poet in *Alastor*, Prince Athanase does not isolate himself from mankind. Athanase is educated not only by books and nature and ruins, but by the wise man Zonoras. He is surrounded by interested if misunderstanding friends. He commits no sin against sympathy. Neither does he pursue a vision; indeed, he is presented in the fragments we possess as partially ignorant of the strange ailment which is destroying him. In Mrs. Shelley's note we find another difference between *Alastor* and the projected conclusion of *Prince Athanase*: Athanase in his search for "the One whom he may love" meets and evidently loves "Pandemos, or the earthly and unworthy Venus; who, after disappointing his cherished dreams and hopes, deserts him" (159). More important is the fact that "Urania, . . . the lady who can really reply to his soul," was to appear in the flesh at the deathbed of the Prince. The odds against Athanase's finding love were evidently not so great as those against the success of the Poet in *Alastor*. This greater potentiality for success may be directly attributed to Athanase's freedom from the sin of un-sympathy. The mysterious sorrow, "strange, and shadowy, and unknown," which plagues him cannot be punishment for a rejection of other human beings as in the case of the *Alastor* Poet. Although his sympathy for "his kind" manifests itself through pity, his pity is not tinged with contempt or pride. Yet,

> . . . like an eyeless nightmare grief did sit
>
> Upon his being; a snake which fold by fold
> Pressed out the life of life, a clinging fiend
> Which clenched him if he stirred with deadilier hold;—
> And so his grief remained—let it remain—untold.
>
> (ll. 120–24, 161)

Shelley's deliberate choice of indirection does not prevent Zonoras from concluding that unrequited love is the cause of Athanase's distress (ll. 232–35, 164). The Prince's reaction to Zonoras' analysis indicates its oversimplification, not its error. Athanase knows that he does not suffer from unrequited love, in the generally understood meaning of this painful condition, because he is not in love with *anyone* who can refuse to return his feeling. There is no object for his love; there is only the void which signals the need of personal love. Zonoras is right and wrong. Erotic passion drives Athanase to become a wanderer in an attempt to escape its destructive force. From the urgency of spring and his own need, Athanase's pure heart, his love of good, his spiritual and psychological freedom offer no protection. His readiness to accept one "who appears to him to embody his ideal of love and beauty" can only be explained by the intensity of his need. The beautiful paean to Love in Fragment VI concludes,

> —the weak
> Alone kneel to thee, offering up the hearts
> The strong have broken—.
>
> (ll. 294–96, 166)

The "weakness" here is similar to that which Shelley assigns to the Poet in *Alastor* when he quotes,

> The good die first,
> And those whose hearts are dry as summer dust,
> Burn to the socket.

Athanase is not a weak character. Shelley takes some pains to indicate his fearlessness and strength (see ll. 43–53, 160). The explanation for this contradiction lies in the virtues which make Prince Athanase a good man, his understanding and sensibility.[8]   His sympathy for others rests on his ability to feel with them. The ability to feel constitutes his weakness as well as his strength. Like all Shelley's heroes, he directs this feeling only toward love. He cannot hate even his enemies; he cannot arm his heart with callousness or selfishness. Therefore, in committing himself to love of Pandemos, he commits himself totally and thus renders himself defenseless and "weak."

Prince Athanase adds to our understanding of eros in Shelley, for his fate shows that avoidance of solitude as well as freedom from the sin of un-sympathy do not exempt one from the experience of the void and the desperate need for love. His only failure is his superiority, which increases his vulnerability and the likelihood of tragedy. Eros is again destructive, but mitigating elements have appeared. First, Athanase does find a flesh and blood woman whom he falls in love with. Second, the "vision" which in *Alastor* could not exist on earth has descended into a body. The problem is shifted from the quest for the impossible to the discernment of the true.[9] Athanase's affair with Pandemos is disastrous, but it is a step in the right direction. The fact that Urania appears, melodramatically too late, at least points to the possibility that somewhere, sometime, such a meeting could take place in surroundings more favorable to the development of a love affair. Erotic passion, produced by the experience of the void, here leads to an object and consequently to eros. Pandemos is the wrong object, but the Prince's involvement with her rescues him from a passion which cannot be fulfilled on earth. This false love destroys him because he is not sophisticated enough to discern its shallow hypocrisy, but it also opens the door to the possibility of finding a true object and the establishing of a relationship of love.

Shelley says in the Advertisement to *Rosalind and Helen* that the poem is "in no degree calculated to excite profound meditation," and a close reading forces one to agree. It is an amazingly bad poem, although Mary Shelley evidently regarded it with favor.[10]

Through Helen the reader is introduced to Lionel, whom we feel we have met before. Unlike his two poetic predecessors, Lionel becomes active in politics in a time which closely resembles the French Revolution:

> But then men dreamed the agèd earth
> Was labouring in that mighty birth,
> Which many a poet and sage
> Has aye foreseen—the happy age
> When truth and love shall dwell below
> Among the works and ways of men. . . .
>   (ll. 602–607, 177)

In the reign of terror which follows, he stands alone as an advocate of reason and love which all, even the "unpersuaded tyrant," respond to. Lionel's actions bewilder men who cannot find any common motive for his daring behavior, yet "all men loved / Young Lionel, though few approved . . ." (ll. 672–73, 178). The villains in the poem are Power, "seated / Safely on her ancestral throne," and Faith, "the python." Eventually slavery and custom are restored. These social events, convenient vehicles for Shelley's attacks on religion and kingship, function more directly in the poem as a background and motivation for the actions of Lionel and clearly delineate his character.

The frustration of Lionel's youthful hope for mankind rather than erotic passion becomes the goad, "a Spirit of unresting flame," which drives him over the "world's vast wilderness." When he returns three years later, he is so changed that no one knows him. The terrible metamorphosis was caused by a love affair much like that between Athanase and Pandemos:

> 'Twas said that he had refuge sought
> In love from his unquiet thought
> In distant lands, and been deceived
> By some strange show. . . .
>   (ll. 756–59, 179)

His melancholy verses, found blotted by tears, describe this second disillusionment in the familiar terms of lack of sympathy:

> "I wake to weep,
> And sit through the long day gnawing the core
> Of my bitter heart, and, like a miser, keep,
> Since none in what I feel take pain or pleasure,
> To my own soul its self-consuming treasure."
>   (ll. 775–79, 180)

Eros has found another victim who like Prince Athanase is unable to discern hypocrisy.

But, unlike Urania in *Prince Athanase*, Helen appears before Lionel's soul and heart are consumed by his bitterness. Her companionship and love heal his mind though his health remains precarious (ll. 812–17, 180). Eros, after its first destructive onslaught, functions now as healer and rejuvenator. In contrast to the previous poems, love, functioning through the character of Helen, is good and a bringer of life. This love is not "Platonic," "And so we loved, and did unite / All that in us was yet divided . . . (ll. 844–45, 181)."[11]

Helen's love and Lionel's response seem to presage a happy ending. This pair of lovers meets the strict demands of Shelley. Then disaster strikes from the outside. Lionel, charged with blasphemy, is imprisoned in a dreary tower. He is finally released for no explainable reason. The imprisonment is fatal, although Lionel and Helen enjoy a blissful reunion and quiet interlude: Lionel dies in Helen's arms.

Before Lionel's death in the temple, which the modern reader cannot help but view as ridiculous in its grotesque sentimentality, Helen sits and plays upon his mother's harp. This scene is remarkably similar to the vision of the veiled lady in *Alastor*, and indicates clearly the differences between the two poems. The lady in *Alastor* is veiled, an unattainable vision created from the Poet's own fancy, and sent as punishment for his lack of sympathy. Helen is flesh and blood, the very accessible lover of Lionel, who succeeds in bringing him happiness and peace though she cannot prevent his death. Eros, in this further development, need not always begin and end in a destructive, illusive quest.

Julian and Maddalo: A Conversation stands far above its predecessors in poetic excellence and its handling of a larger number of characters. The gothic immaturities of *Alastor* are confined and regimented into the functioning device of the madhouse. The sentimental effusions of *Prince Athanase* and *Rosalind and Helen* are incorporated into the poem's structure in a controlled and meaningful context through the ravings of the Maniac.

The significance of this poem to my discussion is in its form rather than its content. *Julian and Maddalo* is not really about love. Taken in its totality, the poem revolves around the question asked by the Maniac, "What Power delights to torture us?" (l. 320, 197). The incident of the Maniac, driven to madness by his love, is the central illustration which draws attention to the theme of the poem, but it is an illustration—the life of Maddalo, the conversation between him and Julian, are others—not the subject. Shelley's ability to construct from the emotions of eros a solid and objective framework indicates a development in his concept of eros as well as his increasing poetic power. The cascade of emotion and suffering pours from the mouth of a Maniac, a sympathetic madman who touches us with pity and tenderness, but a maniac nonetheless. Julian's sincere but glib reliance on man's will—

>   it is our will
> That thus enchains us to permitted ill—
> We might be otherwise—we might be all
> We dream of happy, high, majestical.
> Where is the love, beauty, and truth we seek
> But in our mind?
>   (ll. 170–75, 193)

—founders on the fact of the Maniac's madness. Even he must realize that it is impossible for such a person to "will" his sanity or rationalize his suffering and its effects. "Love, beauty, and truth" are to be found in the mind only in one sense. The mind must conceive love, respond to beauty, and seek truth but the mind is not sufficient in itself—the *Alastor* Poet aptly demonstrated that. The mind which unites the poet (imagination), the philosopher (wisdom), and the lover (sensitivity) is compelled to seek these in a human being outside himself. Just as these qualities made possible that sympathy, pity, and understanding which characterize Shelley's heroes, they also create the need for communication with a being who can share such sympathies and return with understanding the emotion and feeling which constitute their source. When such a relationship exists, as it does between Helen and Lionel, Laon and Cythna, Prometheus and Asia, nothing can do real harm to the lovers. Society may persecute them, religion may martyr them, or Jupiter may separate them; but these disasters imposed by external forces never succeed in destroying what is real and lasting—eros.

The final phase in Shelley's developing concept of eros is presented in *Epipsychidion*.[12] As poetry it is difficult to judge. The tension which the poet creates between what he attempts to express and what is capable of expression is the major unifying quality of the poem as well as the immediate cause of its weakness. Shelley fully realized the difficulty and took rather fanciful pains to direct its "message" to "a certain class of readers." A commentator trying to elucidate the poem must inevitably feel that he, unfortunately, belongs to that larger class to whom "it must ever remain incomprehensible." I am ready to admit at once that I am dull and that it is beautiful.

The poem's first movement is a compendium of ecstatic images in praise of Emily. Because of the unqualified enthusiasm of this praise, most critics interpret this address as Shelley's tribute to the Spirit of Love.[13] They find it impossible to conceive that such extravagance is directed to a living, breathing female. I do not. If the poet's words are read as praises of the Spirit of Love, the poem loses the meaning Shelley is trying so hard to give it. His struggle is to describe the incarnation and real existence of the ideal Love he had so long cherished in his imagination. His later, actual disappointment with Emilia is not relevant to the immediacy of the poem. The wonder and the rare magic in the subject of this poem is that the miraculous has happened. This miracle exists in the poem; if it founders outside the universe of its poetry, that failure is a subject for biographers, not for critics.

My first assumption then, is that Shelley the poet, within the created world of his poem, addresses a real, individual woman. Therefore, the form of the poem differs significantly in its method from those earlier poems already discussed. This is a direct confrontation—the lover telling his beloved of his love. The disasters and wrong choices and suffering are all in the past; they touch the living glory of the present only to fall away as shadowy contrasts. The island paradise will hold only the poet and Emily in spite of his invitations to complementary astronomical bodies. This contradiction is one of many the poem attempts to reconcile. Love for Emily, we are told again and again, does not preclude the poet's love for others; "True Love in this differs from gold and clay," but the projected picture of life on the island makes no mention of *ménage à trois ou quatre.*

The poet strives to make his love spiritual or "Platonic"—"To whatsoe'er of dull mortality / Is mine, remain a vestal sister still"—but the frequent images which convey this desire lead inevitably to that ideal vision of the lovers in their paradise where he promises,

> Our breath shall intermix, our bosoms bound,
> And our veins beat together; and our lips
> With other eloquence than words, eclipse
> The soul that burns between them, and the wells
> Which boil under our being's inmost cells,
> The fountains of our deepest life, shall be
> Confused in Passion's golden purity,
> As mountain-springs under the morning sun.
> (ll. 565–72, 423)

To explain away the physical aspect of this union by calling it a symbolic image of spiritual passion is to destroy the tension which the poem creates.[14] For while the poet's central subject is the realization of his ideal love, failure is woven into the periphery like a refrain. No reconciliation is possible; both opposites, existential realization and inevitable failure, stand side by side in the poem. Although the immediately successful realization is emphasized and dwelt upon, this coexistence is the true "hard matter," the logos of the work. An examination of the various strains of this leitmotif of failure will illustrate my meaning.

The first two stanzas set the pattern of failure and foreshadow the conclusion. The verses are called "These votive wreaths of withered memory" in line 4, and the second stanza picks up and elaborates the image of withered flowers. In line 9, the poet introduces the rose, that familiar image of love; but this rose, the symbol at once of love and of the poem, differs drastically from the traditional image we have come to expect of poets.

> This song shall be thy rose: its petals pale
> Are dead, indeed, my adored Nightingale!
> But soft and fragrant is the faded blossom,
> And it has no thorn left to wound thy bosom.
> (ll. 9–12, 412)

These lines may be read as an assertion of the spirituality of the poet's love. The possible Freudian reading of line 12 only reinforces this interpretation. While not denying such a reading, I choose to emphasize a different aspect of the lines. The rose, love, is dead; it has no thorn to wound; the faded beauty of the blossom exists only in its fragrance. The love described here begins, then, as a dead rose and the varying movements of the poem are so many attempts to revive what has been destroyed. The pattern is not the usual one of fresh, blooming love which must eventually wither and die; Shelley begins where most love poems end and struggles throughout the poem to sustain the revival of what he had abandoned all hope for, the resurrection, through Emily, of the rose. Here is a clue to the basic tension of the poem—the miraculous revival of love from death and the attempt to sustain the new life.

This tension is more obvious in the poet's losing struggle with language, "Ay, even the dim words which obscure thee now / Flash, lightning-like, with unaccustomed glow . . ." (ll. 33–34, 412). The inspiration and power of his love for Emily are the inspiration of the poem just as they are the subjects which he accuses himself again and again of being unable to describe or realize in poetry. The address to Emily ends with a description of the poet's inadequacy:

> . . . —I measure
> The world of fancies, seeking one like thee,
> And find—alas! mine own infirmity.
> (ll. 69–71, 413)

The burned wings of his "moth-like Muse" prevent him from teaching "Time, in his own gray style" all that she is. He is doomed to failure, yet his love and its sunlike influence enable him to escape that doom of time for the duration of the poem. His persistent acknowledgment of inevitable failure functions almost as a charm to ward it off momentarily. Line 123 introduces the second open acknowledgment:

> . . . Ah, woe is me!
> What have I dared? where am I lifted? how
> Shall I descend, and perish not?

The immediate answer is that "Love makes all things equal," but the final answer comes in lines 587–91:

> . . . Woe is me!
> The wingèd words on which my soul would pierce
> Into the height of Love's rare Universe,
> Are chains of lead around its flight of fire—
> I pant, I sink, I tremble, I expire!

Although the envoy in some measure softens the note of triumphant failure just sounded, the voyage appears to be off.

The poem's basic dichotomy is also illustrated in the pervasive

contrast between the cold, common hell of life and the world within
this world built by love. This contrast between two worlds per-
meates the poem so thoroughly that it is likely to go unnoticed.
Emily's "own words" which preface the poem and the envoy which
concludes it indicate that this contrast is a conscious one and an
important part of the poem. The contrast between the world as it
exists and the world created by love serves as foundation for most of
the complimentary images addressed to Emily.

> Sweet Benediction in the eternal Curse!
> Veiled Glory of this lampless Universe!
> (ll. 25–26, 412)

> . . .

> Thou living Form
> Among the Dead!
> (ll. 27–28, 412)

> . . .

> A Smile amid dark frowns? a gentle tone
> Amid rude voices?
> (ll. 62–63, 413)

> . . .

> The glory of her being, issuing thence,
> Stains the dead, blank, cold air with a warm shade
> Of unentangled intermixture, made
> By Love, of light and motion. . . .
> (ll. 91–94, 414)

Life is described in line 187 as a "garden ravaged," and the poet goes
"Into the wintry forest of our life . . ." (l. 249) in his search for love.
The image of life as a forest is sustained throughout the middle
section of the poem until the appearance of Emily in lines 321–34.
However, this basic contrast is not presented as a complete antithesis
between love and life. The poem moves toward synthesis which is
also evident in the imagery. Emily is compared to the Sun, a
part of our world as well as part of Love's rare Universe. The effect
of her entrance into the poet's life is portrayed in natural imagery of
spring; she is

> A Metaphor of Spring and Youth and Morning;
> A Vision like incarnate April, warning,
> With smiles and tears, Frost the Anatomy
> Into his summer grave.
> (ll. 120–23, 414)

The complete synthesis of the world of life and the world of love is described in the imagined relationship of the lovers on the island:

> Possessing and possessed by all that is
> Within that calm circumference of bliss,
> And by each other, till to love and live
> Be one. . . .
>
>   (ll. 549–52, 423)

In the same way the demon of time and its mutability will be metamorphosed into a semblance of eternity:

> I have sent books and music there, and all
> Those instruments with which high Spirits call
> The future from its cradle, and the past
> Out of its grave, and make the present last
> In thoughts and joys which sleep, but cannot die,
> Folded within their own eternity.
>
>   (ll. 519–24, 422–23)

The changes which bring death to the rose lose their fatal power in this setting where time is no longer measured by clocks or decay:

> The spotted deer bask in the fresh moonlight
> Before our gate, and the slow, silent night
> Is measured by the pants of their calm sleep.
>
>   (ll. 533–35, 423)

This eternity in time will eventually yield peacefully to death and a larger eternity:

> Be this our home in life, and when years heap
> Their withered hours, like leaves, on our decay,
> Let us become the overhanging day,
> The living soul of this Elysian isle,
> Conscious, inseparable, one.
>
>   (ll. 536–40, 423)

Shelley is everywhere trying to make life and love one, to reconcile the world of time and change to the world of love and eternity. However, this synthesis takes place only in the hypothetical life of the lovers on the island. The last parts of the poem are put into the form of an invitation. Through this device the poet describes what life *would* be like *if* and *when* the island were reached. The poem does not progress beyond this hypothesis.

The flight and the description of the island present the final attempt at a poetic fusion of the real and the ideal.[15] The island itself partakes of both worlds, and this double nature sometimes makes its location confusing. Shelley probably intended it to be real *and* ideal, for the poem never abandons entirely all hope that such a place could exist somewhere, sometime on this earth. The Paradise image which appeared earlier in the poem—"The wilderness of this Elysian earth" (189)—here becomes fully articulated (see ll. 416–17, ll. 422–23, ll. 425–28, ll. 453–60).

The "lone dwelling" which is the "chief marvel of the wilderness" also possesses a double nature. It was first built "for delight" by some "wise and tender Ocean-King, ere crime / Had been invented, in the world's young prime. . . ." Now, this "pleasure-house" appears not "a wreck of human art" but

> Titanic; in the heart
> Of Earth having assumed its form, then grown
> Out of the mountains, from the living stone,
> Lifting itself in caverns light and high. . . .
>   (ll. 494–97, 422)

This mingling of human art and nature through the medium of time has produced a structure which seems to grow spontaneously from Earth, imaging the inherent perfection which exists potentially in this world. It is Titanic, not Olympian.

Thus, Shelley describes an Eden which might be constructed from the ruins of all those former paradises inherited by man from religion, mythology, or history. It is ideal and so nonexistent; but if it ever comes into being, it will be situated, like the Eden of Adam and Eve which it resembles, on this earth, surrounded by nature at her best. The poet creates a vision of ideal life and love firmly rooted on this earth, not floating in a Heaven of the upper atmosphere. For the duration of the poem, within the eternity of its poetry, the attempt is realized and the miracle exists. What Shelley wants, he wants here, now, although he admits it may be possible only "beyond the grave." When he says, "I never thought before my death to see / Youth's vision thus made perfect . . ." (ll. 41–42), he means that the vision *is* made perfect; Emily is the incarnation. Only three lines later he is wishing again, "Would we two had been twins of the same mother!" His constant return to the existence of imperfection shows an awareness of the actual world that Shelley is unable to ignore.

The dualism that plagues every other aspect of the poem shapes the love of the poet for Emily. Perhaps what Shelley attempts is best described by Denis de Rougemont when he declares that "we must not throw away life with error, but love better. Not extinguish or transcend, but transmute, transfigure!"[16] Just as Shelley transfigured the island into a paradise, so he transfigures Emily and his love for her. There is no extinction nor transcendence, but an incarnation which transfigures.

> See where she stands! a mortal shape indued
> With love and life and light and deity,
> And motion which may change but cannot die;
> An image of some bright Eternity. . . .
> $\qquad\qquad\qquad$ (ll. 112–14, 414)

She is a vision "like incarnate April." In a fragment not used in the poem, she is addressed as "O embodied Ray / Of the great Brightness . . . " (ll. 38–39, 412). She is "Soft as an Incarnation of the Sun, / When light is changed to love" (ll. 335–36, 419). The image of the two meteors in lines 575–79 presents the same idea:

> One passion in twin-hearts, which grows and grew,
> Till like two meteors of expanding flame,
> Those spheres instinct with it became the same,
> Touch, mingle, are transfigured. . . .

The repeated concept of incarnation which these images are built upon tells us all we need to know about who and what Emily is. She is neither the Spirit of Love nor Pandemos. The Spirit of Love is incarnate in her. Like Christ, she is both human and divine, but this double nature should not cause us to slight the human and make her entirely divine. Such action makes the miracle of incarnation meaningless. Because the poem is not wholly successful in reconciling these series of tensions, the reader is easily drawn into the error of reading it on only one of two extreme levels: lusty adultery and free love *or* sublime Italian Platonics. Actually, the poem should be a synthesis of both physical and spiritual love, as the imagery related to Emily easily proves. She is a *mortal shape* indued with love, light, life, and deity. She is an *image,* a concrete instance, of some bright Eternity. When Shelley does speak of Emily as completely divine it is in terms of an antenatal life which would have been preferable to the present existence:

> . . . O too late
> Belovèd! O too soon adored, by me!
> For in the fields of immortality
> My spirit should at first have worshipped thine,
> A divine presence in a place divine;
> Or should have moved beside it on this earth,
> A shadow of that substance, from its birth;
> But not as now. . . .
>   (ll. 131–38, 414–15)

"But not as now" is the lament of the physical, earth-bound Shelley, who despairs of transfiguration in the act of creating it.

The middle of the poem, which deals with the love history of the poet, is a full development of the "plot" we found recurring in fragments throughout *Alastor, Prince Athanase, Rosalind and Helen,* and *Julian and Maddalo.* In *Epipsychidion* all the pieces are fitted together, and we have a dénouement of sorts. There have been significant changes in Shelley's "love story." In contrast to the Poet in *Alastor,* the poet's *spirit,* not the poet himself, met a "Being" on its "visioned wanderings." He does not see her, not even on his "imagined shore," because she is "robed in such exceeding glory." The poet experiences this Being indirectly through nature, through poetry and "high romance," and in

> . . . that best philosophy, whose taste
> Makes this cold common hell, our life, a doom
> As glorious as a fiery martyrdom.
>   (ll. 213–15, 416)

In all these things the Being was "the harmony of truth." She rises from these three earthly sources—nature, literature, and philosophy. She does not descend from some Heaven. Although she passes "like a God throned on a wingèd planet" into the "dreary cone of our life's shade," her birth was mortal.

This loss affects Shelley in much the same way the loss of the veiled lady affected the *Alastor* Poet. Both contemplate suicide. But a mysterious voice directs Shelley to seek his vision on earth: "'O thou of hearts the weakest, / The phantom is beside thee whom thou seekest.'" By accepting the voice, Shelley commits himself to a search *on earth* for the embodiment of his vision. This commitment cannot be abandoned for a leaky boat as it was in *Alastor* when the quest became difficult. So we see Shelley caught in the paradox of the lover without a beloved. He cannot "dissipate / The night which closed on her," nor can he

> . . . uncreate
> That world within this Chaos, mine and me,
> Of which she was the veiled Divinity,
> The world I say of thoughts that worshipped her. . . .
> (ll. 242–45, 417)

Shelley, like the Romantic poet, turns himself toward life, that wintry forest, and begins his long search. Like Satan he must make Hell his Heaven, for that is all he has. And things happen. His encounter with the lady by the well whose voice is "venomed melody" recalls Prince Athanase, Lionel, and the Maniac. She sits *by* the well, which is an image in the poem for inmost being. She does not participate in this image but lurks like a temptation beside it. Obviously, she is sensual love devoid of any other qualities. Her function in the poem is clear. Sensual love alone is deadly; it poisons the well of being rather than feeds and sustains it. In the poem's structure, her appearance is balanced against that of the Moon, which symbolizes an intellectual love stripped of all sensual elements. Neither is sufficient, although the "flame" of the sensual lady is more immediately devastating (see ll. 259–66, 417).

There is no shortage of candidates for the glass slipper, as the poet seeks the shadow of his idol in "many mortal forms." But none will do. He reaches a critical condition when "like a noonday dawn, there shone again / Deliverance." However, that noonday dawn heralded the moon not the sun. The Moon brings light, that much used image in Shelley for love, but it is a cold light. She "warms not but illumines." Obviously, her light is an intellectual one. It lacks the sensual dimension which was the "flame" of the lady by the well. The Moon, accordingly, brings a different kind of destruction. The poet finds himself "within a chaste cold bed"; he is neither "alive nor dead." As soon as he becomes aware of his condition and its deficiency, the relationship is broken. Storms blot out the Moon; and the "Planet of that hour," which I assume is the Comet of line 368 with its accompanying Tempest, brings only temporary relief from his death in life. The images of cold and earthquake multiply and culminate in an extraordinary description of a winter of being. These cosmic images of cold, frost, and winter prepare for the advent, so carefully built up by contrast, of Emily. She enters radiating life, light, and warmth.

The appropriateness of the Sun as symbol for Emily need not be dwelt on. It is clear that she is a synthesis of the lady by the well and the Moon. The Comet prefigured her coming in its combination of light and heat; but the fluctuation and transitoriness, "alternating attraction and repulsion," which characterize the Comet find no place in the permanence and beneficence of the Sun. I previously quoted from Shelley's preface to *Alastor* the tripartite division he habitually gave to human nature: "the intellectual faculties, the imagination, the functions of sense." In this poem we see the movement toward Emily, the Sun, as a slow progress toward the reconciliation of these qualities in one woman. The functions of the sense alone are poisonous flame; the intellectual faculties without the senses are an abnormal life-in-death. The junction of these qualities in the Comet was unsuccessful because they were not organically reconciled. The Comet lacked the "imagination," the unifying quality which the Sun possesses. Emily is the perfect incarnation of that Being which the poet had envisioned from his experience of nature, literature, and philosophy.[17]

The unity of this poem, when it achieves unity, results from the basic tension of what Shelley wishes to express and what is capable of expression. At times the polar opposites which create tension, for example in the portrayal of the human and divine in the poet's love for Emily, are fused successfully; at other times they disintegrate into mere contradictions. This alternation accounts for the specific unevenness of the poem, but in a larger, total view this final inability to achieve perfect synthesis through "incarnation" is the subject and theme of *Epipsychidion*. If we can take this total, we may pronounce the poem a success in spite of its flaws and paradoxes.

Epipsychidion, thus, gives us a complete picture of Shelley's idea of eros. This idea is composed of complex ingredients. It involves the concept of sympathy. The repeated images of mingling and union rely on a sympathetic communion of two like beings. The likeness resides in the mental or spiritual qualities and aspirations which make up the minds and souls of the lovers. There can be no true communication without this community of interests. But Shelley's eros also involves differences—primarily the physical difference between the sexes—which mitigate the narcissistic elements of the relationship. Both these aspects of love are expressed in the following lines:

> We—are we not formed, as notes of music are,
> For one another, though dissimilar;
> Such difference without discord, as can make
> Those sweetest sounds, in which all spirits shake
> As trembling leaves in a continuous air?
> (ll. 142–46, 415)

The need for such a communion of bodies and union of spirits is emphasized by the void which the poet experiences. Each character in the poems I have discussed is faced with the problem of Adam when he surveyed the garden and its creatures but found none like himself. The beauty of nature, the wonder of poetry, and the delight in philosophy ultimately throw into stronger relief the isolation and loneliness of the hero. The fullness of his understanding emphasizes the emptiness of his being. This abyss which opens up within the inmost being must be filled. The *Alastor* Poet succumbed to an idealized erotic passion which could never find fulfillment and led inevitably toward death. Prince Athanase in his pity and charity for others less fortunate than himself found this sympathy an insufficient answer for his unknown suffering. Lionel, disillusioned in his hopes for social reform, sought refuge in a false love without success. The only medicine for this disease which besets each hero is true love. When such a love is not possible, the hero is driven to desperate substitutes which are all doomed to eventual failure. A relationship of love is the sole means of overcoming the void. Thus, eros is of supreme importance to the poetic characters I have discussed. It occupies a central position in the multitude of concepts which find their way into Shelley's thought and poetry.

I indicated previously that a major problem about eros in Shelley's poetry was the disastrous consequences which seemed invariably to follow the footsteps of love. Specifically, the question was the relationship of eros to death. Did Shelley see death as the persistent effect of eros? Did he identify or confuse the two? I believe that these questions can be answered by a brief comparison of pertinent passages concerning death in *Alastor* and *Epipsychidion*.

The movement of the *Alastor* Poet toward death begins shortly after his vision:

> . . . Does the dark gate of death
> Conduct to thy mysterious paradise,
> O Sleep?
>
> . . . .
>
> This doubt with sudden tide flowed on his heart,
> The insatiate hope which it awakened, stung
> His brain even like despair.
>
> (ll. 211–22, 19–20)

He does not, however, despair completely. Immediate suicide would prevent his searching for the vision. But after the quest has proved a vain one, the Poet follows an impulse; he passively yields himself to what seems certain death when he sets sail in the damaged shallop:

> A restless impulse urged him to embark
> And meet lone Death on the drear ocean's waste;
> For well he knew that mighty Shadow loves
> The slimy caverns of the populous deep.
>
> (ll. 304–307, 21)

Death becomes the only passage out of his misery and into a realization of his love:

> . . . The boat fled on
> With unrelaxing speed.—"Vision and Love!"
> The Poet cried aloud, "I have beheld
> The path of thy departure. Sleep and death
> Shall not divide us long!"
>
> (ll. 365–69, 23)

The supreme power and dangerous lure of death is made clear in a line which has the effect of making synonymous love and death:

> . . . as led
> By love, or dream, or god, or *mightier Death*,
> He sought in Nature's dearest haunt, some bank,
> Her cradle, and his sepulchre.
> (ll. 427–30, 24, [italics mine])

In the passage which immediately precedes the death of the Poet,
the narrator addresses death, the "colossal Skeleton," and acknowl-
edges him "king of this frail world." Because this passage demonstrates so clearly the predominant role of death in the Poet's passion
and quest, I quote it in full.

> —O, storm of death!
> Whose sightless speed divides this sullen night:
> And thou, colossal Skeleton, that, still
> Guiding its irresistible career
> In thy devastating omnipotence
> Art king of this frail world, from the red field
> Of slaughter, from the reeking hospital,
> The patriot's sacred couch, the snowy bed
> Of innocence, the scaffold and the throne,
> A mighty voice invokes thee. Ruin calls
> His brother Death. A rare and regal prey
> He hath prepared, prowling around the world;
> Glutted with which thou mayst repose, and men
> Go to their graves like flowers or creeping worms,
> Nor ever more offer at thy dark shrine
> The unheeded tribute of a broken heart.
> (ll. 609–24, 28)

Death is not only mightier than love but a god whose worship has
required, until the death of the Poet, tribute of broken hearts.

The above point of view is in complete contrast to the view
inherent in *Epipsychidion*. In the later poem, as I have said, the
movement is away from death toward a new life. The dead rose will
live again, resurrected by love. The Poet first describes his search
for the Being he loves in a dangerously suicidal image:

> Then, from the caverns of my dreamy youth
> I sprang, as one sandalled with plumes of fire,
> And towards the lodestar of my one desire,
> I flitted, like a dizzy moth, whose flight
> Is as a dead leaf's in the owlet light,
> When it would seek in Hesper's setting sphere
> A radiant death, a fiery sepulchre,
> As if it were a lamp of earthly flame.—
> (ll. 217–24, 416)

But the initial temptation to use death as an escape from the suffering of life is quickly met and avoided:

> I would have followed, though the grave between
> Yawned like a gulf whose spectres are unseen:
> When a voice said:—"O thou of hearts the weakest,
> The phantom is beside thee whom thou seekest."
>   (ll. 230–33, 416)

The perseverance of the poet in his quest and his endurance of suffering lead him finally to Emily and love. There is no ambiguity in this love. Eros not only sustains life, but triumphs over death:

> —the destined Star has risen
> Which shall descend upon a vacant prison,
> The walls are high, the gates are strong, thick set
> The sentinels—but true Love never yet
> Was thus constrained: it overleaps all fence:
> Like lightning, with invisible violence
> Piercing its continents; like Heaven's free breath,
> Which he who grasps can hold not; liker Death,
> Who rides upon a thought, and makes his way
> Through temple, tower, and palace, and the array
> Of arms: *more strength has Love than he or they;*
> *For it can burst his charnel, and make free*
> *The limbs in chains, the heart in agony,*
> *The soul in dust and chaos.*
>   (ll. 394–407, 420, [italics mine])

We may explain this antithesis to the philosophy of love described in *Alastor* in one of two ways. First, we may see this change as a result of Shelley's development toward a mature concept of love, a concept which embraces the difficulty and suffering as a necessary dimension of the arduous search for true eros. A second explanation involves a distinction between the experience of the *Alastor* Poet and the poet in *Epipsychidion*. It is possible to view the experience of the *Alastor* Poet as a commitment to erotic passion in the sense in which De Rougemont defines passion in *Love in The Western World*. Such a commitment is not a search for love, but a desire for death. De Rougemont's analysis of the Tristan Myth can be successfully applied to the Poet in *Alastor*. But *Epipsychidion* deals with love, not a passion for death. Therefore, we may contrast the erotic passion of *Alastor* with the passionate eros described by *Epipsychidion*.

In either case, the positive, beneficent eros of *Epipsychidion* is Shelley's final formulation of the essence and role of love between man and woman—the thread that guides man out of the labyrinth of death into "Love's rare Universe."

GEORGE F. REINECKE

CONRAD'S *VICTORY*:
Psychomachy, Christian Symbols, and Theme

AT LEAST since Albert J. Guerard's *Conrad the Novelist,* it has been unfashionable to discuss the symbolism of *Victory.* Following hard upon the attacks of Douglass Hewitt and Thomas Moser,[1] Guerard's book not only casts doubt upon the very existence of a systematic symbolism in the novel, but denies the book any literary value even if the symbolism exists. His reason is that since the work lacks the essential values of a novel—good story at the literal level, mature and deep characterization, skillful narrative technique, and readable style—no symbolism can save it from rejection as a work of art.[2] This revaluation, though coming in the wake of four decades of praise, is so categorical as to have frightened all but the hardiest of the interpreters of *Victory,* and them it has left suspect.

It is surely not my intention here to reply to a critic of Professor Guerard's standing on so broad a front. Yet, I disagree with him on the following points, and whatever I have to say about *Victory* must assume these disagreements: (1) I find that a systematic symbolism laden with important meaning is the very core of the book, and (2) I think that the value of the book lies in its slow transition from the world of the realistic tale, set in Conrad's conventional East Indian milieu, to a morally simplified microcosm on the island of Samburan. Here, running along with the literal story, I detect a Prudentian psychomachy being acted out, the participants indeed having their roots in real character but also standing for

70

aspects of the contemporary intellectual's mind, as exemplified by Heyst's in the earlier portion of the book. It is this externalized soul-struggle and the implicit conclusions the reader is asked to draw from it which give weight and significance to the tale.

Perhaps Professor Guerard's strictures are in some measure due to his assumption that the rules of genre applicable to the best of early Conrad and to the late nineteenth-century novel generally must be appropriate a priori as criteria for *Victory*. Perhaps the book's involvement with the symbolic (as I read it) should cause us to evaluate it more in the terms of medieval literature on one hand and of later twentieth-century fiction on the other. The term allegory has been carefully avoided here, for Conrad's own "Author's Note" to *Victory* indicates that the chief characters, Heyst, Lena, Jones, Ricardo, Schomberg, all have prototypes in the author's human experience;[3] and I believe the symbolic structure to have grown organically from these experiences, not to have imposed itself coldly in the more usual allegorical manner, even though my allusion to Prudentius should suggest the strong affinities to early religious allegory.

At its simplest level, *Victory* tells of an aristocratic Swede in early middle age, Axel Heyst, who for some time has drifted about the Malayan Archipelago, exploring, observing, but avoiding all involvement, until he unexpectedly arrives in Portuguese Timor at the right moment to relieve the distress of a kindly trader named Morrison, known but slightly to him, whose ship is about to be auctioned off because he cannot pay a minor fine. Somewhat to Heyst's embarrassment, the trader insists on making Heyst a partner. From this association springs the idea for a coal mine and fueling station which will bring the benefits of steamships and the industrial revolution to the Indies. No sooner is the first coal mine well under way than Morrison dies in England and the stock company collapses, leaving Heyst to live hermitlike at the abandoned coal mine, with no company but a Chinese servant.

One of Heyst's infrequent returns to the settlements finds him at Sourabaya, at the hotel of a pompous and evil-tongued German, Schomberg by name, who has, quite without Heyst's knowledge, long disliked him for his aloofness and slandered him concerning his role in the death of Morrison and the bankruptcy of the coal company. Schomberg has arranged for the nightly performances of a traveling all-girl orchestra. Casually, Heyst attends one of their performances and amidst the sordid atmosphere and worse music, is struck by the beauty and freshness of one of the musicians. When he sees her being mistreated by the manageress of the troupe for being unwilling to "circulate" among the customers at the interval, he offers her his help. She admits to near despair, especially in the face of Schomberg's determined advances. Quite spontaneously, he offers to take her away; and with some help from Mrs. Schomberg, they elope to Heyst's island home, leaving Schomberg frustrated and enraged.

A means of revenge comes Schomberg's way when a cadaverous, taciturn individual named Jones, his "secretary," the knife-wielding Martin Ricardo, and their savage South American servant Pedro settle down at his hotel, bully him, and set up an illegal gambling game on his premises. Seeing an opportunity to rid himself of Jones and to punish Heyst, he tells Ricardo an embroidered version of Heyst's supposed betrayal of Morrison, emphasizing the presence of great amounts of money on the island. Ricardo convinces Jones that they should seek to rob Heyst, and they set out in an open boat.

They arrive at Samburan half dead from thirst and are put up rather doubtfully by Heyst, who conceals Lena from them and is watchful, since he can think of no good reason for their presence. The weaponless Heyst feels sure he cannot survive the attack of the three visitors. His plan is to send Lena to the nearby native settlement for whatever protection they can give her. But insincerity between Ricardo and Jones is working against their success (of course their ultimate aim, the treasure, is nonexistent); Jones is a woman hater of a pronounced sort, and Ricardo has kept from him the knowledge of Lena's existence. He has made himself known to Lena, and she conceives the heroic plan of pretending to yield to Ricardo until she can disarm him of his knife. In the rapid series of events at the denouement, all played to the basso ostinato of an erupting volcano in the background, Jones aims at Ricardo to revenge himself for his betrayal when he discovers him with Lena. He kills Lena instead, but eventually kills Ricardo, too, and then presumably drowns himself. Heyst, having understood Lena's love only when it is too late, for he too learned of and misinterpreted her actions with Ricardo, joins her in death on the flaming pyre of their bungalow.

We know that Conrad believed he was doing something quite new when he was in the early stages of writing *Victory*.[4] Surely this originality was not in the setting or plot. The use of the "cleared" stage of Samburan for the simplified action of the last chapters is anticipated by the ship chapters of *Chance*, his previous novel. As I hope to show, there may be something new in the systematic arrangement of the participants in the *psychomachia* on Samburan; it is quite conceivable that the newness (for Conrad) is in the thematic concepts which underlie the melodramatic plot and suggest the system behind the symbols.

Conrad's childhood was spent with his exiled Catholic father, a martyr to the Polish nationalist cause. The novelist's adult life was marked by the abandonment of Poland and the rejection of formal Catholicism (and Christianity).[5] Concerning this last, it may have been too easily concluded in the past that Conrad was therefore necessarily an atheist or agnostic; e.g. "To Conrad the forces controlling the universe were impersonal. . . ."[6] Yet shortly before the writing of *Victory*, Conrad himself gave public expression to belief in a creational teleology, albeit an amoral one:

I have come to suspect that the aim of creation cannot be ethical at all, I would fondly believe that its object is purely spectacular: a spectacle for awe, love, adoration, or hate, if you like, but in this view—and in this view alone—never for despair![7]

The bearing of this philosophical statement on *Victory* can hardly be overemphasized, although there is no certainty that Conrad's view remained static from 1912, when it was published, through 1914–15 when *Victory* was being written.

If we begin with the title itself, "victory" must refer to Lena's disarming of Martin Ricardo. Doubtless there is some irony implied, since her purpose is to make the island safe for her beloved Heyst; yet both he and she die within the hour. The irony may be that the victory is of a moral and spiritual kind not envisioned by her naïveté; if so, this implies a development from the position of the above quotation toward a more traditional ethical view. On the other hand, if the irony implies that there *is* no victory, and that she is deceived, this view would be more in keeping with the quoted statement, but would tend to put Conrad squarely in the camp of the negative pessimists, Heyst père and Mr. Jones, who are without mistake the villains of the piece. Such a conclusion seems unlikely.

There is no doubt that Heyst in the early part of the book is a product of his father's philosophic school. This father's search for truth had ended in a debacle of negation and permanently impressed the son with the belief that the only alternative to utter withdrawal from mankind was the attitude of contemptuous pity. Now in Conrad's system of a few years previous, pity was not a virtue, but an egotistical vice; and we may safely conclude that he disapproves of the kind of pity recommended by old Heyst, though he may have come to distinguish between pities.

If, as I do, one concludes that Conrad's position had shifted to the more traditional and moral one alluded to earlier, then there is a tension between what Heyst believes to be the nature of his pity for the tragi-comic Morrison and the true nature of his response to Morrison's plight and inept gratitude. Later, the reasons Heyst offers himself for becoming involved in the rescue of Lena are equally specious. To some degree, he has been forced into virtuous action in a world where virtue has meaning, yet he goes on denying it to the last chapter. But it is because of Heyst's kindnesses that all the subsequent action is made possible, including those which lead to his unhappiness and eventual death. What has been lacking in Heyst's response is the human emotion of love.

Whereas in the earlier part of *Victory* there are only hints of the later symbolic significance of other characters as anatomized members of Heyst's psyche (e.g., Lena's sobriquet, Alma), from the time he returns to Samburan with Lena, the entire action may be read at one level as representing the conflict of mental faculties (whether *in esse* or *in posse*) characteristic of a particular sort of modern intellectual, of whom Heyst is the embodiment in the novel. Thus, Heyst in one sense expands into the entire personnel of the forthcoming struggle, and in another sense contracts into his own most dominant trait—frigid though well-meaning dominance of the rational faculty to the exclusion of all others. On the same level of interpretation, Lena (Alma) represents the emotions and perhaps the will in their capacity for good. Into the simplified field of action come Mr. Jones and Ricardo, who are Heyst's and Lena's respective opposite numbers. Jones is the personification of negative and evil intellectuality, while his associate represents the capacity for evil present in the will and the emotions.

This horizontal division on the basis of faculties of the mind is completed by the opposition of Wang, Heyst's Chinese servant, to Pedro, Jones's savage ex-alligator-hunter. These two seem to signify the polar extremes of human instinct. Wang, domesticated, married, tilling his acre on the paradisal island, typifies positively directed, and therefore good, instinctive, subintellectual promptings. Pedro personifies the urge to total unrestraint. Note that Wang eventually destroys Pedro in an action prompted by desire to preserve himself and those associated with him (V, 339). Setting up the oppositions and degrees graphically, we arrive at this table of the battlefield of Samburan, or the human mind:[8]

FACULTY	POSITIVE	NEGATIVE
Intellect	Heyst	Jones
Emotions	Lena	Ricardo
Instinct	Wang	Pedro

That this scheme is objectively present in the work and not merely imposed by the reader is implied by several passages in the text. Heyst is normally referred to as "Number One," whereas Jones is "my principal." Ricardo says to Lena, "You and I are made to understand each other. Born alike, bred alike, I guess" (V, 242). The hierarchic division of the faculties of the human mind found above seems based on the Aristotelian and scholastic tradition perpetuated by the Catholic schools of the western world into our own time. It would seem likely that such a division became common to the thinking of Conrad during his school years in Poland or perhaps from the conversation of his intellectual father, since the subject would not normally have been taken up until an age when Conrad was already at sea. Whatever its source, this division of faculties may well be the most important single factor of the book influenced by Conrad's religio-philosophic background.

The one point at which the transition from the ordinary psychological novel to the psychomachy may best be seen is at the last sentence of Part III, chapter v: "He had just felt the clasp of her arms round his neck, when, with a slight exclamation—'He's here!'— she disengaged herself and bolted away into her room" (V, 184).

The blossoming of Heyst into a full human being through union with Lena had just been halted by his learning for the first time of the slander centering on Morrison's death. Though her love for Heyst is so strong as to desire no scrutiny of the story, Heyst is hurt that Lena had not assumed his perfect integrity. Rather, she relied on the power of her total love to cover up any possible guilt. He retires to his father's books in a room presided over by the severe portrait of that polymath. There, the first volume he picks up is his father's final negation of all human values. He reads; soon he feels he is "hearing his father's voice, . . . a ghostly voice. . . . With what strange serenity, mingled with terrors, had that man considered the universal nothingness!" (V, 180–81). Heyst reads from his father's last pages: "Men love their captivity. To the unknown force of negation they prefer the miserably tumbled bed of their servitude. Man alone can give one the disgust of pity; yet I find it easier to believe in the misfortune of mankind than in its wickedness" (V, 181).

In the charged scene which follows, Lena returns from the bedroom and directly asks him to try to love her, and he seems about to yield to emotion: "all his cherished negations were falling off him" (V, 184). But the embrace is interrupted by her cry of "He's here." In the very next paragraph, Jones and his henchmen are sighted off the island; but since nothing of their nature is known, Lena's remark can only refer to her psychic response to the presence of old Heyst's negativism. Yet, since Jones is in the wings, a significant connection is surely intended between old Heyst and the spectral Mr. Jones. Their clothing becomes a symbol of their connection, for only once is allusion made to old Heyst's apparel. He wears an "ample blue dressing gown." Rather improbably, Mr. Jones has brought with him to Samburan an "old but gorgeous blue silk dressing gown." It is this he wears during his final interview with Heyst; a little later it becomes his shroud: "The water's very clear there, and I could see him huddled up on the bottom . . . like a heap of bones in a blue silk bag" (V, 75, 310, 340). We thus have good ground for believing Jones to be an embodiment of the negative attitudes and rejection of humanity that marked old Heyst and remained the chief obstacle to his son's happiness.

Yet, of course, as has been frequently suggested by others, Jones must be associated to some degree with the devil. The very name

Jones is no mere anonym like "Smith" in *Chance;* Davy Jones is the seaman's devil. Jones's conversation abounds in allusions to better times, fallen greatness, and other Luciferian hallmarks; and indeed the faded rich brocade of the dressing gown must suggest the tarnished empyrean blue of a fallen Miltonic angel, carried with him even into the pit. The allusions to Heyst as Adam (V, 141) and the obvious parallels to the pair in the Garden of Eden bear out the notion that the devil is symbolically present.⁹ Even more striking is Jones's mysogyny. Further, it is the very womanhood of Lena which defeats him and yet brings about her own death. This is a clear echo of Genesis 3:15 (Douay), "I will put enmities between thee and the woman, . . . she shall crush thy head, and thou shalt lie in wait for her heel." Tentatively, it may be pointed out that Mary is often called the second Eve in Catholic liturgy and devotional litera-ture; and in iconography she is commonly shown crushing a serpent. Moreover, the sobriquet "Alma," though usually taken as the Spanish for "soul," is also commonly applied to the Virgin in Latin hymns with the sense of "kind, fostering, loving." No strict analogy or identity between Lena and the Virgin Mary is suggested; rather, it is possible that Conrad here too utilized, though less directly, the matter of his childhood religion to give symbolic depth to a state-ment of philosophy of life, and that the role of Mary the Virgin is taken over by the tarnished but redeemed and redeeming, loving life-force, the vitality of sexual love—indeed by Maria Magdalena.

But to return to the adversary, we see that Jones is associated with Satan not merely because they are both evil, but because evil in the Catholic school is so often explained as a negation. The *Catholic Encyclopedia* s.v. "Evil" cites Origen, Augustine, and Thomas Aquinas to that purpose. "Evil according to St. Thomas, is a priva-tion, or the absence of some good which belongs properly to the nature of the creature. . . . It exists not as an objective fact but as a subjective conception. . . . All realities are in themselves good." That Conrad should draw upon this commonplace of his youth seems not unlikely.

Another basic Catholic notion which seems to be utilized in the delineation of Jones, Ricardo, and Pedro is the division of sins into those of the world, the flesh, and the devil. Surely pride and delight in evil for its own sake are, along with the weakness and inaction of negativism, the chief marks of Jones's character. Just as surely,

Pedro can be aligned with the flesh because of his animal nature. As for Ricardo, the problem is more complicated. At first sight, the sins of the world, notably covetousness and envy, suit him well. His ruling passion is gambling. He avoids alcohol, and this would seem to disassociate him from the sins of the flesh. But then how may we explain his desire for Lena? Perhaps the whole pattern of the three sins represents an abandoned substratum of Conrad's plan; on the other hand, it may be allowed to yield when necessary to the more important symbol of Lena as virtuous emotion triumphing over her counterpart. A third possibility, reconciling the two systems, is that if we prescind from the means employed, Ricardo may be said to have followed the good prompting of nature and chosen life over death when he sought Lena. He thus created the situation which brought down his divided house. If this be true, the final chapters would say that even evil passion is a chink in the armor of the greatest sin, the devil's sin, the refusal and denial of life.

Lena dies firm in the belief that she has emerged victorious, saving her beloved. But at the symbolic level her death is the end of human response for Heyst in his role of the rational faculty; his willing acceptance of death immediately thereafter is the only development possible except a reversion to the *status quo ante.* That his death *is an act* must be noted, as must be the survival of Wang (alone among the combattants) with its implied continuity of life after the defeat of evil. Heyst's last words to the providential Davidson over Lena's corpse are, "Woe to the man whose heart has not learned while young to hope, to love—and to put his trust in life!" (*V*, 339). If there is something commonplace about this remark, then there is banality in most of mankind's broadly accepted utterances. In these words, Heyst perceives that it was his own lack of trust, his emotionless intellectualism which put an end to the possibility of happiness for him, for to the extent that he doubted Lena in her actions with Ricardo, he acted the role of Jones. In the broader sense, Lena triumphs over Ricardo and over Jones; but in the narrower sense, Jones has destroyed her for Heyst.

The plea for involvement with the common human condition which culminates the work is also in effect *Victory's* theme. When Conrad arrived at this view, I believe he was moving with the mind of his times, away from the individualism of the nineteenth century to the twentieth's more corporate view. He was also as-

serting a characteristically Romantic faith in the validity and trust-
worthiness of the emotions as a guide to human action.

Although the spiritual warfare may be so complex as to open
Conrad to the charge of oversubtlety, particularly when Heyst is
combatant and battlefield more or less simultaneously, I think
Conrad has offered to the readers of two generations, those willing
to persevere *per aspera*, a tale heavy with character, occurrence, and
symbol, founded on human nature in the Conrad tradition, yet
laden with an interpretation of the human situation in his own
time.

A Note on Names in Conrad

The significance of the names Magdalena/Alma and Mr. Jones
has already been discussed. Katherine Gatch (*SP* XLVII, 90–106)
has suggested that the name Axel is taken from the *Axël* of Villiers
de l'Isle-Adam, where the chief character also commits suicide just
after discovering love. But since in the early drafts, Conrad's
protagonist was named Augustus Berg (H. T. Webster, *PMLA*,
LXIV, 953 ff.), we cannot push this observation too far. "Heyst" I
take to have been suggested by "highest" and to be related to
"Augustus Berg" which, *pace* the egregious remark of one of the
more recent critics, patently does mean something, i.e. "awe-
inspiring mountain." No doubt Conrad thought this link with the
symbolic volcano in the background a little obvious.

Schomberg is apparently a variant of Schaumberg, meaning a
mountain of froth (or scum). Pedro suggests nothing; Ricardo little
more, unless (since his English origin is insisted on) some connection with the economist and hence with wordly goods is weakly
hinted at. "Wang" is the Chinese word for the emperor as intermediary between earth and heaven.[10] Morrison, that fated man,
is perhaps to be seen as the son of death; more probably, the
providential, watchful Davidson is *filius David*. In the early drafts
of *Victory* as seen in the manuscript now at the University of Texas,
Davidson called his ship not "Sissie" but "Celestial" (Webster, as
cited above). Although she has Chinese owners, the ambiguity of
the earlier name is apparent. Whether the "celestial" shipowners are
to be somehow associated with the occasionally providential role
which Wang is called on to play (perhaps in violation of the

hierarchic pattern), I prefer to leave to the ponderings of others, as also the possible association of the Chinese philosophic concepts of *yang* and *yin* with the positive-negative theme of the novel. Only such an association would give significant meaning to the Chinese servant's name.

MALCOLM O. MAGAW

THE CONFIDENCE-MAN
AND CHRISTIAN DEITY:
Melville's Imagery of Ambiguity

As SCHOLARSHIP has repeatedly pointed out, Christian images and
symbols are consistently present and active in the mythmaking
imagination of Herman Melville. The contexts for Melville's pre-
occupation with the Christian myth are numerous. They include
the Fall of Man, the Incarnation, the Gospel Ethic, Baptism, the
Passion (climaxed by the Crucifixion), Resurrection, the Second
Advent, and the Apocalypse. But Melville goes even further: in
many of his symbolic characterizations he assimilates allusions to
the Christian Deity itself. Familiar examples are the suggestively
Christlike roles played by Pierre, Bartleby, and Billy Budd, and the
hint of God in the characterizations of Captain Vere, the lawyer-
narrator of "Bartleby," Plinlimmon, and the White Whale. Each of
these characterizations, moreover, is typically complex and ambiguous since it embodies other allusions besides those to the Christian
Deity and since Melville's imagery is for the most part symbolistic
rather than allegorical. But among his many characterizations
which are allusive to the Christian Deity, none is as complex nor as
provocative as that of the Confidence-Man. Here is a symbol of
Deity whose complexity is greater even than that of Moby Dick;
this observation, I believe, is particularly interesting because these
two remarkable symbols—the White Whale and the Confidence-
Man—bear a significant kinship.

Outside literal context, the referent in *Moby Dick* for Ahab's

81

famous pronouncement to Starbuck that all visible objects are but as "pasteboard masks" could easily apply to the Confidence-Man as well as to Leviathan. Indeed, these two visible objects wear analogous masks. They both embody white, black, and gray imagery. Although Moby Dick himself is literally white, symbolically his whiteness assimilates the black and the grays of his species. By comparison, in his first guise (chs. i–ii) the Confidence-Man appears as a deaf-mute in "cream colors"; moreover "his cheek was fair, his chin downy, his hair flaxen, his hat a white fur one, with a long fleecy nap."[1] In his guise as Black Guinea (ch. iii) he is portrayed as "a grotesque negro cripple, in tow cloth attire and an old coal-sifter of a tambourine in his hand." His "knotted black fleece and good-natured, honest black face [rub] against the upper part of people's thighs as he [makes] shift to shuffle about." In his third and fourth guises—a man with "a long weed on his hat" and a man "in a gray coat and white tie" (chs. iv–viii)—the Confidence-Man displays varied grays which contrast sharply with the deaf-mute's whiteness and the crippled Guinea's blackness. Next, as a "ruddy-cheeked man in a tasselled travelling-cap, carrying under his arm a ledger-like volume" (chs. ix–xv), the Confidence-Man introduces himself as John Truman, the president of the Black Rapids Coal Company. Suggesting the Great Physician, in his sixth guise he appears as an herb doctor, dressed "in a snuff-colored surtout" (chs. xvi–xxi). As the masquerade continues, the Confidence-Man presents himself to the cynical Missouri bachelor in the shabby, darkened tones of a "round-backed, baker-kneed man, in a mean five-dollar suit, wearing, collar-wise by a chain, a small brass plate, inscribed P. I. O.," that is, the Philosophical Intelligence Office (chs. xxii–xxiii). Although his literal description contains no black or gray imagery,[2] this stooped man, wearing a "canine deprecation" and "seeming to wag his very coat-tails behind him, shabby though they were," is a vivid reminder of the crippled, doglike Black Guinea.[3] In his eighth and final guise, the Confidence-Man wears a costume of many brilliant colors: cochineal (red), plaid, flowered, maroon, and royal purple; and the sum of these, it might be said, is objectified in his "white trousers of ample duck" (chs. xxiv–xlv). In this finery of white and its many components, the Confidence-Man declares to all aboard the microcosmic *Fidèle* the universality of his nature: "'A cosmopolitan, a catholic man; who, being such, ties himself to no narrow tailor or teacher, but federates, in heart as in costume, something of the various gallantries of men under various suns. Oh, one roams not over the gallant globe in vain. Bred by it, is a fraternal and fusing feeling'" (151).

The corresponding color imagery in the mask analogy between Leviathan and the Confidence-Man in all his guises objectifies and reinforces their corresponding symbolic meanings: they are both masked images of an unknowable, ambiguous God. In *The Confidence-Man,* from the first to the last chapter, close reading will reveal a curious emphasis on the terms "original" and "original genius"; and their referent is always the Confidence-Man.[4] These terms point to the idea that in the complex imagery of the Confidence-Man Melville is symbolizing the primal force in the universe. Although critics are generally agreed that on a lower level of meaning the Confidence-Man is indeed man,[5] most of them argue that on the higher, symbolic level he is man's perception of Deity. They differ, however, in their interpretations first of Melville's concept of this symbol of Deity and second of his judgment of it. Some argue that the Confidence-Man is another objectification of the Calvinist God; others see him as Christian Deity, but in less restricted terms than those of Calvinism; still others argue that, while he embodies certain allusions to the Christian Deity, the Confidence-Man, like Moby Dick, is too comprehensive and too much the product of Melville's creative, mythmaking genius to be identified exclusively with any traditional concept of God.[6]

In their interpretations of Melville's *judgment* of the God symbolized by the Confidence-Man, critics present theses of negation ranging from restrained skepticism to bitter Timonism. Possibly the clearest statement of the thesis of restrained skepticism is one made by Elizabeth S. Foster in her elaborate and illuminating essay introducing the Hendricks House edition of *The Confidence-Man*: "In *The Confidence-Man* the injurious gods come on stage, in the title role, to get man." The posture of the victim, Miss Foster continues, is "the posture of bafflement, puzzlement, uncomfortable misgiving before the ambiguous smile of the Confidence-Man."[7] Ultimately, "what Melville saw was the need for skepticism. He saw the injury done by all cheating optimisms to man's humanity. . . . One cannot trust God; one cannot trust nature;

but one must cling to some faith in man, for the alternative is too frightful" (lxxxviii–ix).

Merlin Bowen sums up the more negative position taken by those who contend that Melville's Confidence-Man implies a God whose essence is for man altogether unbearable. That God may be unconcerned over the welfare of His creatures, permissive of evil, and sometimes even willfully malicious are possibilities difficult to accept; but, says Bowen, "the most appalling thought is that all our distinctions between good and evil may be unreal in His eyes, that virtue and vice may be no more than 'two shadows cast from one nothing,' and that God Himself, like His universe, may be amoral and all-inclusive. It is just this suggestion of final meaninglessness and absence of all value that makes the phenomenon of whiteness at times so unbearable to Ishmael. . . . [And] it is this [same] unprincipled and chameleon-like God, too unfixed even to merit the epithet 'malicious,' who throughout the bitter masquerade of *The Confidence-Man* diverts Himself by toying, from behind one pasteboard mask or another, with the hopes and fears and weaknesses of mankind."[8]

But regardless of what critical judgment one makes of the God image embodied in the Confidence-Man, two things remain certain: the image is ordered by a mask motif of shifting, symbolic colors and shades; and the extreme complexity of the total image, like that of the White Whale, gives it a meaningful ambiguity.

In Bowen's words, this God is the "Arch Swindler," whose several disguises mark him as a "diddler" of one kind or another and link themselves through the running motif of white, gray, and black. In the white trousers of his last guise, complemented by a mingling of bright hues which are the components of white, the Confidence-Man as the genial cosmopolitan refuses to make any distinction between good and evil. His is the whiteness of neutrality; in his broadmindedness he says that he cannot entertain "any uncharitable prejudice against the rattlesnake" (214). In the eyes of this God of the universe, then, it would seem that virtue and vice have no meaning. Yet Melville lends ambiguity to the moral blankness of the masked cosmopolitan. If virtue and vice have no meaning for him; if in his blankness he is indifferent to the moral arguments of men, then why in the final scene does this God unite with the devil in a conspiracy against a saintly old man to defraud him of both his money and his faith and send him confused and foolish into the blackness of death?

The devil appears in this scene in the guise of a wise and crafty boy peddler with flame-colored garments, sooty face, and a hard horny foot like a steer's hoof (277, 280). But, significantly, his flame-colored garments are matched by the cochineal in the cosmopolitan's harlequin costume. The reds, maroons, and purples, in short, are colors in their own right, as well as the components of white. The cosmopolitan, it follows, wears the colors of the devil along with the apparent whiteness of amorality and neutrality. Moreover, he seems to have certain serpentlike traits himself. In his debate with the mystic stranger on the nature of good and evil (ch. xxxvi), the cosmopolitan speculates on the beauty of the rattle-snake: "'I am pleased to believe that beauty is at bottom incompatible with ill, and therefore am so eccentric as to have confidence in the latent benignity of that beautiful creature, the rattle-snake, whose lithe neck and burnished maze of tawny gold, as he sleekly curls aloft in the sun, who on the prairie can behold without wonder?'" (213). Then Melville's narrator adds, "As he breathed these words, he seemed so to enter into their spirit—as some earnest descriptive speakers will—as unconsciously to wreathe his form and sidelong crest his head, till he all but seemed the creature described." Meanwhile, the mystic asks the cosmopolitan, "'When charmed by the beauty of that viper, did it never occur to you to change personalities with him? to feel what it was to be a snake? to glide unsuspected in grass? to sting, to kill at a touch; your whole body one iridescent scabbard of death?'" The cosmopolitan replies, "'Such a wish, indeed, could hardly occur to ordinary imaginations, and mine I cannot think much above the average'" (213). While this declaration, along with many others, points to the white neutrality of his guise, his later act of conspiracy with the serpent-like boy peddler against the saintly old man demonstrates the cochineal evil of the Confidence-Man's present guise and the black and gray evil of his earlier guises. Melville hints again at the hypocrisy of the Confidence-Man when the cosmopolitan speaks of himself as continually going up and down the world, "'from Teheran to Natchitoches,'" sipping, tasting, and smacking his lips over "'that good dish, man'" whether "'served up à la Pole, or à la Moor, à la Ladrone, or à la Yankee'" (151).

Behind the white mask of neutrality and broadmindedness, then, one sees in the cosmopolitan's image what is *apparently* his real essence—the cochineal and darkened tones of evil. Yet I cannot believe that Melville intends to define the essence of the Confidence-Man explicitly, even here at the end of the novel. As the microcosmic symbol of the God of the macrocosm, the Confidence-Man in all his guises remains forever an enigma, a visible object whose masks are many layers deep—each layer consisting of just another appearance, another illusion, that man himself has attributed to his concept of God. Since for Melville the essence of God cannot be comprehended by man, any attempt to penetrate the masks, the white blankness, can result only in illusion. It is *man* who imputes benevolence or malevolence to the Confidence-Man, and these qualities are merely projections of man's own love or hate, faith or fear. The God objectified by the Confidence-Man is, in the final analysis, hated, feared, or held suspect by most of the passengers aboard the *Fidèle* who put their confidence in one of his masks. But their judgments of these masks are built upon illusions which they have subjectively formed in their own minds. They impose upon these masks a doctrine of morality that is man-made, not absolute. Indeed, from one point of view, the real God of the universe—whatever He may be—becomes for these men a scapegoat for their own inadequacies, foibles, and lack of good judgment. One has only to consider the things they have put their confidence in: herbs, easy chairs, nature, boys, coal companies, Indian charities, counterfeit detectors, and chamber stools. When their faith in these things brings disappointment or disaster, they fail to acknowledge that the cause is largely the error of their own judgment. Instead, they blame the Confidence-Man, whose masks they *think* are evil. Victims of their own illusions, they interpret a God whose masks, for Melville, remain forever uninterpretable. Thus, while Melville's tone in *The Confidence-Man* is certainly sympathetic toward man, it is at the same time critical of man. The tone, like the imagery of the Confidence-Man's many guises, is ambiguous.

The very atmosphere of the novel, it seems to me, amplifies the ambiguity of tone, imagery, and meaning. The steamboat *Fidèle*, says the narrator, leaves St. Louis, bound for New Orleans, on April Fool's Day, a day when men impute illusory meanings to masks that are not what they appear to be. The Fool's Day motif establishes an atmosphere of unreality, fantasy, and dream that is sustained throughout the novel. James E. Miller, Jr., elaborates on this point effectively: "The device of the steamboat sailing down the Mississippi offers something more than a means for bringing together for brief periods of time the various types of humankind. The slow but steady flow of the river, the constant coming and going of the people, the stopping and starting of the boat in its long journey—all suggest not only the flux of life but also the world of fantasy, the world of dream. . . . The reader becomes increasingly aware that the rhythmical flow of the swindling masquerade not only has the unreal quality of dream but even the unsettling impact of the comic nightmare. It is as though the repressed spiritual history of America (or of mankind) escapes from the unconscious and insists on realistic recognition."[9]

The central figure in this dream world is the Confidence-Man, a God whose many-colored masks are the fantastic projections of the minds of those men who unconsciously turn to dreams and illusions to give themselves identity. Until they relate themselves to an external object, they cannot have a self-conscious identity. Thus in their dream world, which for them is the only reality, they seek a God in whom they can place their confidence. But, for men in a dream world, whatever God they may conceive of must be as much a part of that dream world as the men themselves. He becomes, then, an ambiguous composite of moral, immoral, and amoral masks, each of which mirrors the illusory images of man himself. Although the Confidence-Man is a symbolic representation of God, for the finite mind he can only be a man-God, a God who can be perceived only insofar as he is somehow identifiable—usually unconsciously—with the perceiver. Without a concrete, visible object on which to focus, the finite mind cannot perceive. In the dream world of the *Fidèle*, therefore, men may *think* that they are perceiving a God of reality as they fix their eyes upon the Confidence-Man. They may *think* that they can see amorality behind his white mask, or evil behind his black mask; but all "perceptions" in the fantasy of life are illusions. The masks are not removed; they are only replaced by other masks. Melville closes his fantasy with the impact of understatement when he says, "Something further may follow of this Masquerade."

In creating his many-masked symbol of this ambiguous man-God,

Melville the artist evokes from traditional myth the image of another man-God—Christ. But, while this complex image embodies allusions to Christ, at no time is there a direct analogy between the two, and at no time is the allusiveness to be interpreted as a basis for theological argument. The Confidence-Man is *not* an allegorical symbol of God the Son. The composite of many allusions, the Confidence-Man is a mythical God in his own right; and, while the few allusions to Christ which Melville blends into the imagery of the Confidence-Man are significant, they are not exclusive. They are only parts of an elaborate symbol whose total meaning must remain forever ambiguous if it is to unite organically with the theme of Melville's fantasy.

In all eight of his guises the Confidence-Man embodies allusions to Christ. One of these allusions is suggestive and detailed, two are remote, and five are relatively clear and unimaginative.

The blonde deaf-mute (ch. i), the first of the eight confidence men, embodies a more detailed allusiveness to Christ than any of his seven successors. "A man in cream-colors," he first appears "at the water-side in the city of St. Louis. . . . He was unaccompanied by friends. From the shrugged shoulders, titters, whispers, wonderings of the crowd, it was plain that he was, in the extremest sense of the word, a stranger" (1). He appears to be "evenly pursuing the path of duty, lead it through solitudes or cities"; and in his aspect there is a singular innocence as he writes on his slate, " 'Charity thinketh no evil, . . . Charity suffereth long, and is kind, . . . Charity endureth all things, . . . Charity believeth all things, . . . [and] Charity never faileth' " (2–3). The passengers regard him as a "simpleton" whose "lunacy . . . was heightened by his muteness, and, perhaps also, by the contrast to his proceedings afforded in the actions—quite in the wonted and sensible order of things—of the barber of the boat" (3). This barber, "jumping on a stool," hangs over his door "a gaudy sort of illuminated pasteboard sign" bearing the words " 'No Trust' " (4). The crowds have been reading a poster offering a "reward for the capture of a mysterious impostor, supposed to have recently arrived from the East" (1); but no one apparently identifies the deaf-mute with the impostor. Meanwhile, the unobtrusive "simpleton" retires inconspicuously to the foot of a ladder and reposes: "though he might not have a long way to go, yet he seemed already to have come from a very long distance," from "some far country beyond the prairies" (5). And, "gradually overtaken by slumber, his flaxen head drooped, his whole lamb-like figure relaxed, and half reclining against the ladder's foot, lay motionless, as some sugar-snow in March, which, softly stealing down over night, with its white placidity startles the brown farmer peering out from his threshold at daybreak" (5). "From his betaking himself to this humble quarter," moreover, "it was evident that, as a deck-passenger, the stranger, simple though he seemed, was not entirely ignorant of his place . . ." (5).

Unlike all the other characters in *The Confidence-Man* this singular figure is associated with an almost exclusive whiteness. And since it is the assimilation of all colors, his symbolic whiteness embodies several meanings simultaneously. In its most comprehensive context the stranger's whiteness designates him as the unknowable God of the universe. His deafness and his muteness, moreover, amplify this particular aspect of his ambiguity, for they apparently prevent any direct communication between him and the passengers. And if the passengers cannot communicate with him, they cannot identify themselves with him. Thus they regard him with a momentary curiosity that soon lapses into indifference. Indeed they are as indifferent toward him as it appears he is toward them. Although for them he is a *visible* object and has the physical outlines of a man, as a deaf-mute he is only a half-man and therefore not to be taken seriously. For a man can take seriously only himself and those objects in which he sees himself mirrored. And no man is likely to think of himself as a half-man. Thus, when he attributes lunacy to someone, he does it condescendingly or in jest, and with no more than a passing interest. Ironically, a man is unconsciously denying the existence of Divinity in his own being, then, when he evaluates this half-man as *less* than a man instead of *more* than a man. Thus, because the referent to all of a man's serious conceptions is limited to his own image, what the passengers aboard the *Fidèle* regard as the reality of this man-God's whiteness is just another of the many illusions that they create for themselves in their dream world. In effect, the whiteness of the deaf-mute is symbolic not only of the unknowable God of the universe but also of the opaque masks which men themselves—unable to do anything else—impute to God.

Among these masks is the Christian God, objectified in Christ, who is Himself an ambiguous composite of masks imputed to Him by men. As symbolist and mythmaker, Melville borrows the Christ image from tradition and assimilates it creatively into the complex imagery of his own mythical God—the Confidence-Man. This method of borrowing and reshaping images and then assimilating them into his own symbolic images brings into focus a quality of eclecticism quite fundamental to Melville's art. And what is most significant, this method unites itself with Melville's basic meaning: the ambiguities of appearances. A technique that is characteristically eclectic lends itself to unlimited suggestiveness and therefore to an extreme degree of ambiguity in its imagery.

Although in the total image of the Confidence-Man there are eight basic masks which collectively embrace Melville's intended ambiguity on a broad, comprehensive level, each individual mask contains an ambiguity peculiar to itself. There are, to be sure, far more than eight dimensions of ambiguity in the total image of the Confidence-Man. Since the deaf-mute derives more implicitly from the figure of Christ than from any other source in Melville's imagination, the ambiguity of this first mask points in part to an admixture of unreconcilable and similarly ambiguous perceptions men have held about the model, Christ.

Unlike his seven successors, the deaf-mute does not practice a confidence game; he does not fleece any of the passengers on the *Fidèle*. In the words of Miss Foster, "he commits no wrong, except perhaps unintentionally in softening victims for subsequent swindlers, and in no way, except to some people through his oddity, suggests that he is an impostor. . . . He seems 'singularly innocent,' gentle, helpless, and harmless. Though banged and nearly overthrown by some of the porters, though jeered and buffeted by his fellow Christians, he remains meek, gentle, dreamy. In this world he is, 'in the extremest sense of the word, a stranger'" (l-li).[10] Like Christ and Paul, he brings the essence of the Christian ethical message to the world. But because of his muteness it would seem that he cannot actually communicate with mankind, and because of his deafness it would seem that he is out of touch with the needs of humanity. For he communicates his Gospel in words traced on a slate, which he carries "shield-like" before him, and he remains apparently insensitive to the jeers and epithets of the crowd. Finally, his position by the stairs leading upward suggests that the way to heaven, to salvation, is through Christ. Moreover, in his essay on *The Confidence-Man* James E. Miller, Jr., observes that "details such as the flaxen hair, which might suggest the eunuch or sterility, indicate the major and recurring theme on which Melville is about to embark in the *Fidèle*: the inapplicability to this world of heaven's law. This theme or its variation appears in all of Melville's work—in *White Jacket*, for example, in the vignette of the 'murderous' but praying canoneer; and in *Pierre* in the Plinlimmon pamphlet's distinction between chronometrical and horological times (or ethics). Like *Pierre, The Confidence-Man* is a major treatment of the theme. Throughout it is demonstrated over and over again, in a constantly shifting context, that Christ's heavenly doctrine of charity (love) is unworkable, at least in any absolute sense, among human beings on earth—primarily because it does not take into account the very real presence of evil (the devil)."[11]

But, while all of these meanings may be suggested, they are presented in a context of ambiguity that denies them the conclusiveness attributed to them by Miss Foster, Miller, and a number of other critics. Not only the deaf-mute, but also the barber communicates his message, " 'No Trust,' " in the inaudible language of symbols; yet the passengers respect him, and many of them endorse his philosophy even though they never enter the barber shop to hear him defend his position. Those who do communicate with him directly find that he has very little to say and that his positiveness makes him almost as deaf to their questions and reasonings as the deaf-mute appears to be. Ultimately, the passengers' respective judgments of the deaf-mute and the barber *could* both be wrong. If on the one hand they accept the message of the barber's sign and on the other disregard or even reject the message of the deaf-mute's sign, it could be reasoned that their choice is not altogether a defensible one—that, in fact, it is founded on a propensity for skepticism that is possibly no more reasonable in its argument than an endorsement of faith might be. In relation to the total meaning of *The Confidence-Man*, what this implies is that men in their dream world will hear and believe what they want to hear and believe. Their judgments of masks—whether they be masks of barbers, deaf-mutes, herb doctors, cosmopolitans, or all the others —are inspired by illusions that may be either near or far from the truth. From this point of view, then, it is they who impute deafness and muteness to the Christlike stranger who is the first of the eight confidence men.

Moreover, since illusions are essentially the reflections of the men who create them (men can identify others only in terms of themselves), the deafness and the muteness of the stranger are ironically a mirror of the passengers themselves; these apparent handicaps are not an intrinsic part of this symbolic man-God's nature (or if they are, the passengers have no way of knowing it). It is the passengers in their world of illusions who are actually inarticulate on the subject of Christian love and faith; it is they who are deaf to its message. The true Christ, insofar as He corresponds to Melville's symbolic man-God, is somewhere behind that ambiguous white mask with its appearances of strangeness, meekness, helplessness, innocence, gentleness, indifference, and incommunicability. And if He becomes an object of men's superficial scorn and negation, it is not His doing; it is theirs. Likewise, if the barber with his "gaudy sort of illuminated pasteboard sign" captures their unrefined imaginations and subsequently wins their affirmation, it is substantially less his doing than it is their own. Yet it is no more Melville's intention to blame men for making questionable choices than it is to blame Deity for being incomprehensible. The question of "blame" is irrelevant, since, as a symbolist who designs his images to suggest multiple and apparently irreconcilable meanings, Melville refrains from making final judgments. His ambiguous symbols carry with them a corresponding and all-inclusive ambiguity of tone and meaning.

The comprehensiveness of Melville's ambiguity in *The Confidence-Man* is more impressively dramatized, significantly, in the central images of the first and the last chapters than anywhere else in the novel. However misguided and unjust the passengers may seem to be in their scorn of the Christlike stranger in Chapter One, neither they nor anyone else can ever know to what degree they are to be held responsible for their own illusions, or indeed how far from truth their illusions may be. As fallible human beings whose very nature denies them the powers of perception ultimately necessary to find reality, they are perhaps as helpless as they are guilty; thus they are presented in an equivocal tone that holds blame and sympathy in balanced suspension. The same evaluation can be made of the dramatic interplay of speech and action between the cosmopolitan and the saintly old man in the final scene of the novel. In their world of illusions most men—but not Melville—have imputed fraudulence and hypocrisy to the motley-clothed cosmopolitan, the defender of Charity. How close they may be to the truth that lies behind his mask no one will ever know. Thus, when the saintly old man puts his confidence in the cosmopolitan and allows himself to be led away into darkness, most men would regard his choice as foolish rather than wise. But they could be mistaken. Melville's ambiguity is as evident on the last page as it has been throughout the novel; no final distinction is made between appearance and reality:

> "Ah, my way now," cried the old man peering before him, "where lies my way to my state-room?"
> "I have indifferent eyes, and will show you; but, first, for the good of all lungs, let me extinguish this lamp."
> The next moment, the waning light expired, and with it the waning flames of the horned altar, and the waning halo round the robed man's brow; while in the darkness which ensued, the cosmopolitan kindly led the old man away. Something further may follow of this Masquerade.

Since the cosmopolitan is a symbol of God, his "indifferent eyes" could imply the power of "disinterested," unillusioned perception, as well as an "indifferent" air in the sense of "uninterested." Thus, when this God promises to show the old man the way, it will probably lead not to the familiar state-room with its many illusions, but rather into a darkness whose meaning Melville leaves ambiguously inconclusive—the darkness of evil, perhaps; or the darkness of the unknown, a darkness beyond which should lie a new light of revelation and reality. The lamp which the cosmopolitan extinguishes, therefore, could represent the light of illusion, as well as the light of goodness or faith. "The waning flames of the horned altar," pictured in the glass lamp shade, could represent the dimming out of man's illusion of evil (Hell), as well as the darkness and finality of death after painful sacrifice. And, in its juxtaposition with the flaming altar on the lamp shade, the "waning halo round the robed man's brow" could suggest the dimming out of man's illusory mask of self-glory, as well as the capitulation of righteousness to evil.

The tone, like the imagery and meaning of this closing scene in the novel, is ambiguous. Toward the saintly old man the tone contains an admixture of comic ridicule, compassion, and affirmation; and toward the cosmopolitan, an admixture of denunciation, sophisticated disinterestedness, and glorification.

To return now to the second and subsequent guises of the Confidence-Man and to explore these for their allusiveness to the man-God of the Christian myth, there is no question that in the imagery of the second guise—namely, Black Guinea, the cripple who begs for money (ch. iii)—there is very little that is reminiscent of Christ. His blackness and his undignified demeanor give him the appearance of the devil. In the dramatic scene in which a man (Melville describes him as possibly a "discharged custom-house officer") questions the truth of Black Guinea's apparent deformity, there is, however, a remote allusion to both the high priest Caiphas's and Pilate's arraignment of Christ.[12] The analogy continues, moreover, when, as in the instance of Pilate who delivered Christ over to the Jews, the arraignment of Black Guinea is transferred from the "custom-house officer" to the "people" aboard the *Fidèle*. After this man retires, Melville writes, "the rest, finding themselves left sole judges in the case, could not resist the opportunity of acting the part: not because it is a human weakness to take pleasure in sitting in judgment upon one in a box, as surely this unfortunate negro now was, but that it strangely sharpens human perceptions, when, instead of standing by and having their fellow-feelings touched by the sight of an alleged culprit severely handled by some one justiciary, a crowd suddenly come to be all justiciaries in the same case themselves . . ." (12). A young Episcopal clergyman, "in a long, straight-bodied black coat," asks Black Guinea, " 'But is there not some one who can speak a good word for you?' " While not a tight analogy, this scene calls to mind the Jews' interrogation of Christ during the Passion. And it helps to reinforce the ambiguity of Black Guinea in his role of confidence man. Whether this suggested image of the harassed Christ is blurred into the cripple's to lighten the apparent evil of his total being is left an open question. The tone could be ironic as reasonably as it could be sympathetic. And if ironic, it would intensify rather than lighten the apparent evil of Black Guinea's guise.

Perhaps even more remote is the possible allusion to Christ in the image of John Ringman, the man with a weed, mourning the death of his estranged wife Goneril (chs. iv–v, xii). In Chapter Five there

is a faint allusion to images of King Agrippa and the Apostle Paul—
and thus, by association, to Christ—when the confidence man, John
Ringman, at the conclusion of a long discourse, asks the sophomore
who reads Tacitus, " 'Could you now, my dear young sir, under such
circumstances, by way of experiment, simply have confidence in
me?' " Paul's words to Agrippa, recorded in Acts 26, suggest a
similar plea for confidence—specifically, confidence in Christ: " 'For
the king knoweth of these things, before whom also I speak freely:
for I am persuaded that none of these things are hidden from him;
for this thing was not done in a corner. King Agrippa, believest
thou the prophets? I know that thou believest.' " Although the
sophomore cannot articulate an answer to Ringman's question, his
manner indicates both inclination and hesitation to respond in the
affirmative: "Somehow, the stranger fascinated him. Little wonder,
then, when appeal came, he could hardly speak, but, as before
intimated, being apparently of a retiring nature, abruptly retired
from the spot, leaving the chagrined stranger to wander away in
the opposite direction" (30). Similarly, Agrippa replies to Paul,
" 'Almost thou persuadest me to be a Christian.' And when he had
thus spoken, the king rose up. . . .' " And, like the confidence man
who wanders away in the opposite direction, Paul soon thereafter
leaves Palestine and goes to Italy. Although the correspondence is
not direct, Paul does act as the spokesman of Christ; thus, by association, one can hear the voice of Christ echoed in John Ringman's plea to the sophomore. The implication seems to be that the
sophomore is wise in turning away from the confidence man. But
no one can be certain of this, since it is man himself who imputes
evil to the confidence man; as symbol of God of the universe, John
Ringman's real essence must remain unknowable.

The five guises of the Confidence-Man which contain relatively
clear and unimaginative allusions to the Christian man-God are
characterized primarily by their embodiment of cardinal Christian
virtues: The man in a gray coat and white tie, agent of the Seminole
Widow and Orphan Asylum and promoter of a project named the
World's Charity, represents Righteousness and Charity (chs. vi-
viii). John Truman, the president of the Black Rapids Coal Company, who encourages men to make speculative investments,
represents Faith (chs. ix–xi, xiii–xv). The herb-doctor, promoting
his Omni-Balsamic Reinvigorator and Samaritan Pain Dissuader,

represents Hope (chs. xvi–xxi). The man with the brass plate, executive of the Philosophical Intelligence Office (chs. xxii–xxiii), and the cosmopolitan (chs. xxiv–xlv) both represent Charity.

Miss Foster finds in these five masks, as well as in those of the other confidence men, "not only philosophic satire but also ironic reference to parts of the Sermon on the Mount and I Corinthians 13. . . . The Negro is one of the meek and the poor in spirit; the man of feeling is one of them that mourn. . . . And they are all spurious" (lvi). Much of the novel, Miss Foster contends, "dramatizes, as a religious allegory, the last verse of the chapter of first Corinthians with which the novel began: 'And now abideth faith, hope, and charity'" (lvi). Implied in the confidence men who represent these virtues are the figures of Christ and the Apostle Paul, who is a type of Christ. Although on one level it may be true that *The Confidence-Man* can be regarded as a religious allegory in which all the confidence men are "spurious," as Miss Foster argues, on the higher level the novel is much more than this. Each mask worn by the Confidence-Man is symbolic, not simply allegorical; and what may appear to be spurious in any given mask is in itself an illusion that only lends ambiguity to the original mask. As a relativist and as a disinterested artist, Melville stands apart from this masquerade which he has fashioned out of a multiplicity of mythical allusions stored up in his imagination. While some of those allusions come from the Christian myth, they are not so clearly the reproduction of their original, nor are they so exclusive of other allusions, that they justify the reader's classifying either the novel or its central God-symbol as Christian allegory dramatized in a context of simple irony.

As visible objects which are but illusions of reality, then, these particular confidence men—whose guises in part hint at Christ and the cardinal Christian virtues—are more comprehensive and inclusive than the limited meanings prescribed by allegory. They are symbols whose ambiguity suggests more profound implications than those of a simple dichotomy.

While their relationship to the Christian myth appears primarily in their objectifications of the cardinal virtues, all five of these confidence men also embody other allusions to the same myth. The man in a gray coat, like Christ, is a carpenter. He has built his Protean easy chair "in odd intervals stolen from meals and sleep"

(43). Moreover, he "revealed a spirit of benevolence which, mindful of the millennial promise, had gone abroad over all the countries of the globe . . ." (46). And the power of his oral delivery is comparable to that of Christ during His ministry: "A not unsilvery tongue, too, was his, with gestures that were a Pentecost of added ones, and persuasiveness before which granite hearts might crumble into gravel" (47). Also the tradition of Christ and His bride, the Church, is implied when the man in a gray coat quietly asks a woman in the ladies' saloon, " 'Madam, pardon my freedom, but there is something in that face which strangely draws me. May I ask, are you a sister of the Church? . . . It is very solitary for a brother here. . . . I find none to mingle souls with. . . . I cannot force myself to be easy with the people of the world. I prefer the company, however silent, of a brother or sister in good standing. By the way, madam, may I ask if you have confidence? . . . Could you put confidence in *me* for instance?' " (49). Later the confidence man leaves the woman with these words: " 'Yea, you can say to me as the apostle said to the Corinthians, "I rejoice that I have confidence in you in all things" ' " (50).

John Truman, like Christ, ministers unto the thirsty. The water he brings to the suffering miser who cries, "Ugh, ugh—water!' " is the symbolic water of spiritual regeneration, and it could suggest the waters of baptism. During the long colloquy in which Truman attempts to win the miser's confidence, he sometimes expresses himself in words that remind one of Christ: " 'My humble profession, sir. I live not for myself; but the world will not have confidence in me, and yet confidence in me were great gain. . . . Downright confidence, or none. So help me heaven, I will have no half-confidences' " (43, 44).

The herb-doctor, analogous to Christ the Great Physician, argues that man's health—and this can be taken symbolically as spiritual health—comes from "divine nature" (91); and, like Christ, he attributes his healing powers to God rather than to himself: " 'When I hear that health is yours, I will not, like some I know, vainly make boasts; but, giving glory where all glory is due, say, with the devout herb-doctor, Japus in Virgil, when, in the unseen but efficacious presence of Venus, he with simples healed the wound of Aeneas:—"This is no mortal work, no cure of mine, / Nor art's effect, but done by power divine" ' " (94).

The man with a brass plate objectifies not only the cardinal virtue of Charity but also a God-like intelligence that makes his discernments of mankind seem omniscient. Looking down as it were from his Philosophical Intelligence Office high up in the hills of Cincinnati, he tells the Missouri bachelor, " 'I have had more or less favorable opportunity for studying mankind—in a business way, scanning not only the faces, but ransacking the lives of several thousands of human beings, male and female, of various nations, both employers and employed, genteel and ungenteel, educated and uneducated; yet—of course, I candidly admit, with some random exceptions, I have, so far as my small observation goes, found that mankind thus domestically viewed, confidentially viewed, I may say; they, upon the whole—making some reasonable allowances for human imperfection—present as pure a moral spectacle as the purest angel could wish. I say it, respected sir, with confidence' " (135).

Finally, there is the cosmopolitan. His mask, faintly allusive to Christ, is the most elaborately delineated of all eight. The cosmopolitan discourses at length on Charity among a wide variety of people and in a variety of contexts, but none of these are directly associated with the Christian myth. In the final chapter Melville draws an analogy between the comely old man and Simeon: he had "a countenance like that which imagination ascribes to good Simeon, when, having at last beheld the Master of Faith, he blessed him and departed in peace" (273). But it is inconclusive that the old man looks upon the cosmopolitan symbolically as his "Master of Faith" when he says to him toward the end of their conversation, " 'Then, good-night, good-night; and Providence have both of us in its good keeping' " (285). Like Christ, the cosmopolitan sees in the universe "a ruling principle of love" and "a ruling principle of kindness" (178). But the wine-drinking episode between the cosmopolitan (Francis Goodman) and his "boon companion" Charles Arnold Noble (chs. xxix–xxx) is, if anything, a perversion of Christ's administering of the Holy Sacrament to his Twelve "boon companions." Thus, while his multicolored costume and his complex character constitute an assimilation of the guises of the seven confidence men before him, the cosmopolitan calls to mind very little imagery of the mythical God-the-Son. Likewise there is very little in his mask that recalls the image of Satan.

Among the many critical essays on *The Confidence-Man*, I have found none whose interpretation of the book agrees with mine. Although some critics recognize elements of ambiguity in the novel's complex study of appearance and reality, none of them regard the all-inclusive meaning as ambiguous. The mask imagery, with its many ironies, they find, is essentially the embodiment of a Christian allegory, an argument which implies that Melville was unequivocally convinced of the rightness and stability of his ideals and that he entertained no doubts about the truths he envisaged. Moreover, their arguments imply that the allusiveness in Melville's imagery is insufficiently imaginative and suggestive to give his symbols the uniqueness and comprehensiveness necessary for the creation of a new myth-world. I cannot agree. The Confidence-Man is a symbolic God in his own right; he is not the Christian God, nor, when all his masks are assimilated, is he a close approximation. Richard Chase, although he does not regard *The Confidence-Man* as an original myth, argues that it is a mistake to interpret the novel as a Christian allegory. This part of his interpretation I find useful, though not altogether consistent with my own: "The fact that the confidence man displays certain Christlike traits in the later parts of the story seems to me less important than the striking fact that when he appears actually to be Christ, he has been *put to sleep* by the author. This I take to be an overt gesture of dismissal of the confidence-man-as-Christ from the conscious, meaningful, and discussable levels of the book. The Christ in Melville's unconscious mind, the 'sleeping Christ,' as we have called him, had great influence on Melville's works. But it is a mistake to make Melville more explicitly Christian than he actually was."[13]

While Melville's allusions to Christian Deity—expressly to God made manifest in His Son—are integral parts of the total image of the Confidence-Man, they do not ultimately define Melville's own mythical symbol of God. These allusions merely lend suggestiveness to the many masks of a symbol so complex and comprehensive that it cannot be defined. And that, in short, is Melville's point. If God is unknowable, then the artist must make his imagery of Him ambiguous. And with ambiguity of meaning must come a corresponding ambiguity of tone—in short, a mingling of sympathy and censure expressed toward the illusioned passengers aboard the *Fidèle*.

WILLIAM E. DOHERTY

TENDER IS THE NIGHT AND
THE "ODE TO A NIGHTINGALE"

CRITICS OFTEN EXPRESS a feeling that there is something mysterious about Fitzgerald's *Tender Is the Night,* that there is something unsatisfying in the analyses we have had—a discomfort one does not feel with the more elaborately structured *The Great Gatsby,* or with the intriguing, unfinished *The Last Tycoon.* Searching the critical opinion on *Tender Is the Night*—this "magnificent failure"—one is likely to feel that something *is* missing; one seems to have, as Maxwell Geismar says, "the curious impression at times that the novel is really about something else altogether."[1]

It seems strange that the relationship between the novel and Keats's "Ode to a Nightingale," which supplied Fitzgerald with both title and epigraph, should have received no more than passing attention from the critics. The epigraph reads:

Already with thee! tender is the night,

. . .
But here there is no light,
Save what from heaven is with the breezes blown
Through verdurous glooms and winding mossy ways.

We know that Fitzgerald had a lifelong and deep response to Keats: "for awhile after you quit Keats all other poetry seems to be only whistling or humming." The "Ode to a Nightingale" was especially important to him; he found it unbearably beautiful, confessed he read it always with tears in his eyes.[2]

100

It is true that the title *Tender Is the Night* was chosen late in the extended course of the book's writing; but it seems clear that Fitzgerald was conscious of the "Ode" not merely in the last stages of composition. The title is appropriate, though no one has said why. Yet, a moment's reflection will show that there is a good deal of Keatsian suggestiveness in *Tender Is the Night* in both decor and atmosphere—the Provençal summers of sunburnt mirth, the nights perfumed and promising, the dark gardens of an illusory world. But I suggest that there are parallels more significant than those of color and mood. The correspondences I offer in this case, when taken individually, might seem no more than coincidental; but considered in their cumulative weight, they indicate a calculated pattern of allusion beneath the literal surface of the novel which deepens the psychoanalytic rationale and adds context to the cultural analysis the book offers. In addition, the "Ode" appears to provide us with a sort of thematic overlay which clarifies unsuspected symbolic structures, essential to the understanding of the book.

I will begin with an admission that weakens my case. Fitzgerald dropped a reference to the nightingale from his second and subsequent versions of the published novel. In the *Scribner's Magazine* version he wrote of "roses and the nightingales" that had become an essential part of the beauty of that "proud gay land," Provence.[3] Why that observation was dropped, I cannot say; but its appearance, however brief, suggests that like Keats, Fitzgerald associated the south of France with the romantic bird. There is a second and more interesting reference which remained. It too connects the bird and the south of France. To understand its significance, one must consider it in context.

The Riviera, Mediterranean France, came to be, as Maxwell Geismar has pointed out, that apogee of ease and grace, that "psychological Eden" in which Fitzgerald and his heroes took refuge.[4] None of his characters responds more fully to this environment than does Rosemary, coming as she does from the "salacious improvisations of the frontier." At the party at the Villa Diana, no guest is more enchanted by the life that seems promised there; she feels a sense of homecoming, feels drawn as if by magnetic lights. The spell of the party is still on her as she lies awake in her room "sus-

pended in the moonshine, . . . cloaked by the erotic darkness." She
is disturbed by secret noises in the night: an "insistent bird" sings
in the tree outside. She is not sure what bird it is, but the singing
and the Divers seem to merge in her mind: "Beyond the inky sea
and far up that high, black shadow of a hill lived the Divers. She
thought of them both together, heard them still singing faintly a
song like rising smoke, like a hymn, very remote in time and far
away."[5] But Rosemary is confused by it all; she cannot think as yet
except through her mother's mind. Abe North identifies the bird for
her:

> "What are *you* doing up?" he demanded.
> "I just got up." She started to laugh. . . .
> "Probably plagued by the nightingale," Abe suggested and
> repeated, "probably plagued by the nightingale" (42).

The entire chapter, heavy with night imagery, seems to lead up to
this identification. Rosemary has been brought up with the idea of
work. Now she is on a summer's holiday, an emotionally lush
interval between two winters of reality; and what she discovers is a
world remote, romantic, something southern, a mysterious dark lure
of life to which she responds—symbolized by the night bird. It is
unreal; a duel will be fought; "up north the true world thundered
by."

What I suggest is that the novel deals with characters who are
plagued by the nightingale, those enamoured of the romantic
illusion. Nicole seems to be the Nightingale.

Consider the scene in which Nicole sings to Dick. As she waits
for Dick at the sanatorium, singing surrounds Nicole, summer songs
of ardent skies and wild shade. The night, the woods, gardens,
flowers are associated with Nicole throughout the novel. Here, the
unknown seems to yield her up, "as if this were the exact moment
when she was coming from a wood into the clear moonlight" (135).
Dick responds to that illusion, wishes that she had no other background, "no address save the night from which she had come." She
leads him to a secret copse. In this melodious plot she has hidden
a phonograph. She plays for him "thin tunes, holding lost times and
future hopes in liaison." Through song the two of them are transported out of the copse into another world. The journey is chroni-
cled in ironic song titles. Finally Nicole herself sings to Dick.

She supposes he has heard all these songs before. " 'Honestly, you don't understand—I haven't heard a thing.' Nor known, nor smelt, nor tasted, he might have added" (136). Now here was this girl bringing him the essence of a continent, "making him a profound promise of herself for so little. . . . Minute by minute the sweetness drained down into her out of the willow trees, out of the dark world" (136). But there is danger in the promise of this "waif of disaster," in the song of this "young bird with wings crushed."

The brief transport from the world which the "Ode" details, the emotional adventure of climax and decline is suggested in this and in a number of other scenes in *Tender Is the Night*. Indeed, the pattern describes the very rhythm of the novel. The party at the Villa Diana, as Malcolm Cowley suggests, appears to be the high point in the story. The scene marks a change of mood; thereafter, the light romantic atmosphere is dispelled.[6] We see there the Divers at their point of greatest charm—a "vision of ease and grace," commanding all the delicacies of existence. It is a high point for another reason. It is in this scene that the principals of the story make an escape from the prosaic and temporal world. In the rarified atmosphere of the party a moment is caught in which a delicate triumph over time is achieved.

The party is given out of doors in the garden, Nicole's garden. To Rosemary the setting seems to be the center of the world: "On such a stage some memorable thing was sure to happen" (29). The guests arrive under a spell, bringing with them the excitement of the night. Dick now seems to serve Nicole as prop man, arranging the set, dressing the trees with lamps. The guests are seated at Nicole's table:

There were fireflies riding on the dark air and a dog baying on some low and far-away ledge of the cliff. The table seemed to have risen a little toward the sky like a mechanical dancing platform, giving the people around it a sense of being alone with each other in the dark universe, nourished by its only food, warmed by its only lights. And, as if a curious hushed laugh from Mrs. McKisco were a signal that such a detachment from the world had been attained, the two Divers began suddenly to warm and glow and expand, as if to make up to their guests, already so subtly assured of their importance, so flattered with politeness, for anything they might still miss from that country well left behind. Just for a moment they seemed to speak to everyone at the table, singly and together, assuring them of their friendliness, their affection. And for a moment the faces turned up toward them were like the faces of poor children at a Christmas tree. Then abruptly the table broke up—the moment when the guests had been daringly lifted above conviviality into the rarer atmosphere of sentiment, was over before it could be irreverently breathed, before they had half realized it was there.

But the diffused magic of the hot sweet South had withdrawn into them—the soft-pawed night and the ghostly wash of the Mediterranean far below—the magic left these things and melted into the two Divers and became part of them (34–35).

When we consider the care with which Fitzgerald dresses this scene, we sense an emphasis beyond what the mere events of the party would demand. This garden, the fireflies riding on the dark air, the summer evening, the wine-colored lanterns hung in the trees—the Romantic decor is there, and the Keatsian atmosphere: "the diffused magic of the hot sweet South . . . the soft-pawed night and the ghostly wash of the Mediterranean far below." There is no need to insist that these images have their antecedents in the "Ode" —in its "murmurous haunt of flies on summer eves," or its "warm south," its "tender night," its "charmed magic casements opening on perilous seas"; for the clearest parallel to the poem lies in the brief achievement of the precious atmosphere, achieved through the familiar Romantic formula of escape at the moment of emotional pitch—here ironically, a moment of social ecstasy, but suggesting inevitably the dynamics of the sexual event. The imagery itself reiterates the pattern: the fragile loveliness of Nicole's garden increases "until, as if the scherzo of color could reach no further intensity, it broke off suddenly in mid-air, and moist steps went down to a level five feet below" (26).

It seems unlikely that the material of the "Ode" was so immediate in Fitzgerald's mind that it would come to add to the novel a dimension of allusion of which he was unaware. We are willing to concede unlimited conscious subtlety to his contemporaries in the novel; but Fitzgerald, despite the evidence of his deliberate workmanship, is too often pictured by critics as a somewhat fatuous tool of the muse, whose mind was inferior to his talent. The intricacies of *Tender Is the Night* would suggest otherwise. Not only is the pattern of the momentary climax a repeated one in the novel; there occurs, too, the *recall to reality* that marks the ending of the "Ode." In the novel it is not the sound of a bell that signals the descent from bliss—or the word "forlorn" striking like a bell, tolling the poet back to his sole self; it is another sound heard three times in the book: when Dick falls in love with Nicole, when Abe leaves on the train from Paris, and when Tommy becomes Nicole's lover. Each time a shot is heard, a loud report that breaks the illusion, signifies the end of happiness and the escape from self.

After Nicole leaves the sanatorium, Dick tries to avoid her; but she fills his dreams. Their chance meeting in the Alps ends in Dick's complete surrender of self: "he was thankful to have an existence at all, if only as a reflection in her wet eyes" (155). As in all her love situations, Nicole is triumphant, self-controlled, cool: "I've got him, he's mine" (155). The scene remains tender; it is raining, the appropriate weather for love in Fitzgerald's novels. But, "suddenly there was a booming from the wine slopes across the lake; cannons were shooting at hail-bearing clouds in order to break them. The lights of the promenade went off, went on again. Then the storm came swiftly . . . with it came a dark, frightening sky and savage filaments of lightning and world-splitting thunder, while ragged, destroying clouds fled along past the hotel. Mountains and lakes disappeared—the hotel crouched amid tumult, chaos and darkness" (155–56).

This is not the storm of passion. Dick has come suddenly to his senses: "For Doctor Diver to marry a mental patient? How did it happen? Where did it begin?" The moment of passion and illusion is over. He laughs derisively. "*Big* chance—oh, yes. My God!—they decided to buy a doctor? Well, they better stick to whoever they've got in Chicago" (156). But Dick has committed himself to Nicole. His clear sight comes too late, and when the storm is over her beauty enters his room "rustling ghostlike through the curtains."

A loud shot sounds the ominous recall another time, in the Paris railway station. Here is departure and farewell; a gunshot cracks the air. Abe, on the train, waves good-by, unaware of what has happened. The shots do not mark the end of his happiness, for he has long been in misery, though they do forebode his violent death. It is the brief summer happiness of Dick—won in a desperate bargain with the gods—that is ending. It marks the end of a summer mirth for the Divers' group, the beginning of misfortune for Dick. Dick and his friends move out of the station into the street as if nothing had happened. "However, everything had happened—Abe's

departure and Mary's impending departure for Salzburg this afternoon had ended the time in Paris. Or perhaps the shots, the con-
cussions that had finished God knew what dark matter, had termi-
nated it. The shots had entered into all their lives. . ." (85).

The third of these recalls to reality occurs just after Tommy possesses Nicole. The entire account from the arrival of Tommy at the
Villa Diana to the departure from the hotel presents a curious
parallel to the ending of the "Ode." Tommy comes to Nicole like
a worshipper before a mystery. His happiness intensifies: "And, my
God, I have never been so happy as I am this minute" (294). But
the time of joy is brief; the point of greatest happiness is a moment
outside of self, a taste of oblivion. The ecstasy passes; disappointment and foreboding follow: "the nameless fear which precedes all
emotions, joyous or sorrowful, inevitable as a hum of thunder
precedes a storm." After the act, things begin to look tawdry to
Tommy. He is edgy and apprehensive. Outside there are disturb-
ing noises: "There's that noise again. My God, has there been a
murder?" The final recall is heard. As they leave the room "a sound
split the air outside: Cr-ACK-Boom-M-m-m! It was the battleship
sounding a recall. Now, down below their window, it was pande-
monium indeed. . ." (296–97). There is a rush to depart. Cries and
tears are heard as the women shout farewells to the departing
launch. The last ludicrous moments of the scene, the girls shouting
their tearful good-byes from the balcony of Tommy's room, waving
their underwear like flags, appear to be Fitzgerald's ironic counterpart to the adieu of the final stanza of the poem. The fading
anthem of the "Ode" becomes the American National Anthem: "Oh,
say can you see the tender color of remembered flesh?—while at the
stern of the battleship arose in rivalry the Star-Spangled Banner"
(297).

II

The title of the novel and the epigraph Fitzgerald offers illumi-
nate the significance of "night" and "darkness" in the story. An
enquiry reveals a complicated and careful symbolic structure in
Tender Is the Night involving a contrast between the night and the
day, darkness and light. The title of the novel declares that the
night is tender. There is in it an implicit corollary about the day.

Early in the story, the sun is established as something harsh and painful, even maddening. The sun troubles the Divers and their group. They seek shelter from it under their umbrellas which "filter" its rays. At the beach the sea yields up its colors to the "brutal sunshine." Rosemary retreats from the "hot light" on the sand. Dick promises her a hat to protect her from the sun and to "save her reason." In the scene in which Nicole lapses into madness at the Agiri Fair, "a high sun with a face traced on it beat fierce on the straw hats of the children." The day scenes are those of pain and fear: "the April sun shone pink upon the saintly face of Augustine, the cook, and blue on the butcher's knife she waved in her drunken hand" (265).

On the other hand, darkness and the night are addressed in fond, in honorific terms: "the lovely night," the "soft rolling night," the "soft-pawed night," the "erotic darkness." Fitzgerald's description of Amiens reveals something of the character and virtue of the night: "In the daytime one is deflated by such towns . . . and the very weather seems to have a quality of the past, faded weather like that of old photographs. But after dark all that is most satisfactory in French life swims back into the picture—the sprightly tarts, the men arguing with a hundred Voilàs in the cafés, the couples drifting, head to head, toward the satisfactory inexpensiveness of nowhere" (59). Part of the meaning is here, but the symbolism of the night is not merely opposite in meaning to that of the day; it is more complicated and more intricately woven into the story. The night is the time of enchantment, masking the ugliness of reality that the day exposes. The night, as in the "Ode," is the time of beauty and the time of illusion. Dick and his friends prefer the night: "All of them began to laugh spontaneously because they knew it was still last night while the people in the streets had the delusion that it was bright hot morning" (79). But the night is not entirely superior to the day. The desirable night is the all allowing darkness. It is a dimness preferred, perhaps, by those ineffective in dealing with the practical day-lit reality. If the day is harsh, it has vigor; the night is the time of ease and also weakness. Some hint of these sinister implications may be detected in the scene in which Baby Warren makes her frustrated effort to aid Dick after he has been beaten and thrown into the Roman jail. She cannot function in the real world: "She began to race against the day; sometimes on the broad avenues she gained but whenever the thing that was pushing up paused for a moment, gusts of wind blew here and there impatiently and the slow creep of light began once more" (227). She cringes at the unstable balance between night and day. The strange creature she encounters in the embassy, wrapped and bandaged for sleep, "vivid but dead," appears an unwholesome figure of the night, incongruous with the day.

It would appear that Fitzgerald has divided his world into two parts—the night and the day. The day is reality, hard, harsh, and vigorous; the night is illusion, tender, joyful, but devitalizing.

The most significant illusion that the night fosters is the illusion of happiness. To the Romantic, happiness consists in preserving the high moment of joy. He has a dread of endings. *Tender Is the Night* is a book of endings: "Things are over down here," says Dick. "I want it to die violently instead of fading out sentimentally" (37-38). Paradoxically, the Romantic dream is that the moment of joy can be embalmed forever in the final night; death then appears to be a welcome extenuation of the night, ending all endings. Both the poem and the novel deal with these lovely illusions; but what they teach is that the fancy cannot cheat so well, that disillusionment is the coefficient of time.

There is a difference in tone between the two works which is due to the fact that Keats emphasizes the swelling dimension of the ecstatic experience, while Fitzgerald deals more with its deflation. Where Keats conveys a sense of disappointment, fond regret, Fitzgerald expresses a Romantic's anti-Romantic argument; for in tracing the grim disenchantment Fitzgerald underscores the sense of deception, trickery, the sense of victimage in the martyring of the dreamer. The "immortal bird" of the "Ode" becomes the "perverse phoenix" Nicole; the deceiving elf becomes the "crooked" Nicole, one of a long line of deceivers, pretending to have a mystery: "I've gone back to my true self," she tells Tommy; ". . . I'm a crook by heritage" (292). We suspect complicity in her father's sin; he tells the doctor, "She used to sing to me" (129).

There are other victims of the Romantic deception—the inmates of the sanatorium where Dick labors without accomplishment. "I am here as a symbol of something" (185), the American woman artist tells Dick. She and the others are there because "life is too tough a game" for them. Unlike the thick-ankled peasants who can take the punishment of the world on every inch of flesh and spirit, these are the fine-spun people suffering private illusions, their "compasses depolarized." They are "sunk in eternal darkness," people of the night, spirits sensitive and weak, now caught in Nicole's garden. For it is Nicole who has designed the means of holding these inmates fast. With floral concealment and deceptive ornament she has created those camouflaged strong points in which they are kept. Outwardly these houses are attractive, even cheerful, screened by little copses; but "even the flowers lay in iron fingers." Perhaps the "Ode" suggested the names: the "Beeches" and the "Eglantine."

III

These inmates are, many of them, the "victims of drug and drink." There is in *Tender Is the Night* what might be called a potion motif, involving liquor, drugs, and poison. As in the "Ode" these are associated with the illusory adventure. Dr. Diver is as much an addict as his patients. In the early parts of the novel wine is associated with the delicacy of living the Divers maintain and with the sensual qualities of their lives. The enjoyable swim in the ocean is like the pleasure of "chilled white wine." The wine-colored lamps at the Villa Diana give a lively flush to Nicole's face. Nicole is gay-spirited after the "rosy wine at lunch." There is a faint spray of champagne on Rosemary's breath when Dick kisses her for the first time. But wine quickly loses its pleasant character. As Dick's esteemed control begins to slip and he acts for the first time without his customary "repose," he stares at the shelf of bottles, "the humbler poisons of France—bottles of Otard, Rhum St. James, Marie Brizzard. . . ." Dick's Roman debauch recalls Abe's disastrous drunks. At home Dick drinks brandy from a three-foot bottle. He comes to regard liquor as food, descending to the level of the rich ruins he treats. Late in the novel we see that the sinister qualities of these draughts, potions, beakersful are associated with Nicole: in falling in love with her, in marrying her, Dick "had chosen the sweet poison and drunk it." Again Nicole is characterized as the attractive evil, the sinister allurement.

The draught of vintage from the deep delved earth, the dull opiate, the hemlock of Keats's poem may not be the direct sources of Fitzgerald's images; yet the associations of drug, drink, and poison with the Romantic appetencies are interesting and suggest that Keats and Fitzgerald were dealing with a similar psychological syndrome—the urge to "fade away, dissolve and quite forget. . . ."

This urge, as Albert Guerard, Jr., points out in his essay, "Prometheus and the Aeolian Lyre," is really the urge toward loss of self, the impulse toward self-immolation, to the drowning of consciousness—one of the hallmarks of the Romantic temperament—which accepts the myth of a vital correspondence between man and nature, a correspondence demanding the submersion of our rational, coherent selves. In the "Ode to a Nightingale," Mr. Guerard argues, Keats has written a poem about the actual submersion of consciousness, dramatizing the process itself, and presenting in the poem a symbolic evasion of the actual world:

In one sense this ode is a dramatized contrasting of actuality and the world of the imagination, but the desire to attain this fretless imaginative world becomes at last a desire for reason's utter dissolution: a longing not for art but for free reverie of any kind. . . . This sole self from which Keats escapes at the beginning of the poem, and to which he returns at its close, is not merely the conscious intellect aware of life's weariness, fever, and fret, but truly the sole self: the self locked in drowsy numbness, the self conscious of its isolation. . . .[7]

Mr. Guerard's analysis may be modified, perhaps, to this degree: the "Ode" seems not so much a product of the Romantic myth of a prevailing correspondence between man and nature as it is an acknowledgment that the correspondence does not prevail. This thesis is reiterated in *Tender Is the Night*. What the nightingale symbolizes and promises in the "Ode," Nicole symbolizes and promises too. The ecstatic union with the bird is a taste of oblivion in loss of self.

Dick manifests the symptoms that Mr. Guerard indicates. There is the obsessive awareness of isolation that characterizes Dick even in his student days. He feels separated from his "fathers." He has the feeling that he is different from the rest, the isolation of the scientist and the artist—"good material for those who do most of the world's work"; but it is a loneliness he cannot endure. He wanted to be good, to be kind; he wanted to be brave and wise; but, as we learn toward the end, "he had wanted, even more than that, to be loved" (302). He gives a strange answer to Franz's criticism of his scholarship: "I am alone today. . . . But I may not be alone to-morrow" (138). One by one he burns his books to keep warm. In marrying Nicole he abandons his work in "effortless immobility." The critics have frequently noted the self-sacrificial aspect of Dick's behavior; but too frequently that self-sacrifice has been taken as the very theme of the novel because Dick gives himself so completely in serving others that he is left with nothing in the end. Rather, this self-sacrifice should be understood as one of the paradoxical impulses which constitute the desire to submerge the self. Self-immolation seems to contradict the longing for freedom from burdens and cares, yet both urges are aspects of the desire to abandon individuality. Abe, like Dick, has a strong desire for loss of self, and forgetfulness. Abe wants oblivion and seeks it in drink; he longs for death. Tommy too has inclinations toward the moribund, following death and violence all over the world. Baby Warren "relished the foretaste of death, prefigured by the catastrophes of friends" (172). Dick looks fondly at death in his decline. At the railing of Golding's yacht he comes close to suicide and to taking Nicole with him. The isolation Dick feels as a young man is never relieved. The entire age is alien to him. Dick mourns on the battlefields of World War I: "All my beautiful lovely safe world blew itself up here with a great gust of high explosive love" (57). Coming home to bury his father, he feels the final tie has been broken; there is no identity with his own land; he feels only a kinship with the dead: "Good-by, my father—good-by, all my fathers" (205).

IV

Finally, what does the correspondence between the novel and the "Ode" reveal about the social and cultural analysis Fitzgerald offers in *Tender Is the Night?* The distinction between the night and the day that Fitzgerald establishes symbolically has its significance in the "class struggle" he presents; the social antagonisms seem to be aspects of the antipathy which arises between the Romantic and the anti-Romantic disposition.

Fitzgerald, as we have seen, divides things into opposing pairs in *Tender Is the Night.* When Rosemary arrives at the Riviera beach she finds two groups. The McKisco party is made up of McKisco, the *arriviste* who has not yet arrived, his silly ambitious wife, two effeminates, and the shabby-eyed Mrs. Abrams. They are pale, gauche people, unattractive beside the Divers' group. The Divers are rich, cultured, talented, leisured. We get a fuller understanding of what these groups may represent in the scene in which Dick and Rosemary visit the house on the Rue Monsieur. It is a place of incongruities and contrasts. Clearly there is a clash between the past and the present, suggesting it seems, the evolving future of the Western world: "It was a house hewn from the frame of Cardinal de Retz's palace in the Rue Monsieur, but once inside the door there was nothing of the past, nor of any present that Rosemary knew. The outer shell, the masonry, seemed rather to enclose the future so that it was an electric-like shock, a definite nervous experience, perverted as a breakfast of oatmeal and hashish, to cross that threshold . . ." (71). The people within are an odd mixture. They fit awkwardly into the environment. They lack the command over life that earlier ages managed to exert. Rosemary has a detached "false and exalted feeling" of being on a movie set. No one knew what the room meant because it was evolving into something else. It is important to recognize who these people in the room are:

These were of two sorts. There were the Americans and English who had been dissipating all spring and summer, so that now everything they did had a purely nervous inspiration. They were very quiet and lethargic at certain hours and then they exploded into sudden quarrels and breakdowns and seductions. The other class, who might be called the exploiters, was formed by the sponges, who were sober, serious people by comparison, with a purpose in life and no time for fooling. These kept their balance best in that environment, and what tone there was, beyond the apartment's novel organization of light values, came from them (72).

The room apparently holds the society of the West. We find in it the McKisco group, the sponges, the hard practical people; and there are the Divers' type, the dissipated old "quality" class, the run-down Romantics who are doomed. The sober and serious exploiters set the tone for the future, and in it they will succeed. Rosemary stands between the two groups. Her youth and success separate her from the Divers' crowd, but she inclines toward them by temperament and training. She is a product of her mother's rearing, tutored in the values of the old society. "I'm a romantic too," Rosemary tells Dick. Yet, she is coldly practical, "economically . . . a boy not a girl." The first day on the beach Rosemary does not know which group is hers. She is attracted by the Divers' party;

but, "between the dark people and the light, Rosemary found room and spread out her peignoir on the sand" (5–6).

The people of the McKisco type are not the victims of Nicole; they are immune to the Romantic illusion. The "tough minded and perennially suspicious" cannot be charmed. McKisco is the only one at the party at the Villa Diana who remains unassimilated, un-affected by the emotional excursion. In the house on the Rue Monsieur there are others who are likewise immune. The "cobra women" discuss the Divers:

"Oh, they give a good show," said one of them in a deep rich voice. "Practically the best show in Paris—I'd be the last one to deny that. But after all—" She sighed. "Those phrases he uses over and over and over—'Oldest inhabitant gnawed by rodents.' You laugh once."

"I prefer people whose lives have more corrugated surfaces," said the second, "and I don't like her."

"I've never really been able to get very excited about them, or their entourage either. Why, for example, the entirely liquid Mr. North?" (72–73).

The incapacity for illusion gives these people an advantage in the world. McKisco, for whom the sensual world does not exist, ends successful and honored; his novels are pastiches of the work of the best people of his time. "He was no fool about his capacities—he realized that he possessed more vitality than many men of superior talent, and he was resolved to enjoy the success he had earned" (205). McKisco's duel with Tommy symbolizes the clash between the two groups and underscores the anachronism of the soldier and hero. Tommy is a product of the older civilization, educated in for-gotten values. Ironically it is McKisco who is "satisfied" in the duel. He builds a new self-respect from his inglorious performance. Tommy, Abe, and Dick are Romantic remnants, the children of another century, fettered by its illusions—"the illusions of eternal strength and health, and of the essential goodness of people; il-lusions of a nation, the lies of generations of frontier mothers who had to croon falsely, that there were no wolves outside the cabin door" (117).

They are the salt of the earth—charming, gifted people, but over-matched in the struggle against the cold, shrewd frauds who are inheriting the earth. *Tender Is the Night* deals with the passing of the old order, with the passing of an attitude toward life, or rather with the last remnants of that life, "the oldest inhabitants gnawed by rodents." The specific content of the illusions which fetter them is less important than how Fitzgerald deals with the attraction to the irrational dream which marks the romantic temperament, a dream which may promise the world, the sustained ecstasy of love or the satisfactions of oblivion—symbolized by the beautiful mad woman, Nicole. She is the dream without real referent. She has no existence outside the mind of the dreamer: "When I talk I say to myself that I am probably Dick. Already I have even been my son, remembering how wise and slow he is. Sometimes I am Doctor Dohmler and one time I may even be an aspect of you, Tommy Barban. Tommy is in love with me . . ." (162).

In the end it is Doctor Diver who is "cured" when he releases her from his mind; he returns to the terrible emptiness of the "sole self." Late in the novel Nicole sings to him again in her "harsh sweet contralto." But this time Dick will not listen: "I don't like that one" (290).

The dream and the dreamer are, of course, Fitzgerald's subject matter in fiction; and in treating them he invariably delivers up the dreamer as victim of his own Romantic infatuations. And yet for all his insight, his self-lacerating satire, Fitzgerald leaves the dream and the dreamer somehow inviolable at the end. Gatsby, that most extravagant Romantic, leaking sawdust at every pore, is still intact at the end and dies with his dream intact. "No—Gatsby turned out all right at the end; it was what preyed on Gatsby, what foul dust floated in the wake of his dreams" that defeated him.

The best of the Romantic writers are not vulnerable to their own myths. The "Ode to the Nightingale" declares exquisitely the abandonment of faith in the imagination. It is not until *Tender Is the Night* that Fitzgerald abandons that last comfort of the Romantic, the notion that the botching, the disappointment of the imagination's most cherished ambitions may be blamed on the unworthy environment of the dreamer. *Tender Is the Night* is a harder, harsher book than *Gatsby;* and it tells us that the super dream is an internal corruption, a damaging, self-begotten beauty. Dick's final return to his sole self in upstate New York—"almost certainly in that section of the country, in one town or another"—is an utterly unsentimental fade-out; the hero is gone from the stage before we can cover him with our fond sympathy, before we can murmur, "Alas."

KENNETH HOLDITCH

ONE MAN'S INITIATION:
The Origin of Technique in the Novels of
John Dos Passos

One Man's Initiation, John Dos Passos's first novel, is significant in illustrating that early in his career the novelist was employing in an embryonic form some of the methods that were later to culminate in his best work. Already he was concerned with several of the problems which would ring out in all his work for forty years. The central idea revolves around the paradox of war: war is pointless, an "agreement for mutual suicide and no damned other thing,"[1] but it continues and cannot be prevented. Already he sees war as nothing more than an instrument for the advancement of capitalism or some other oppressive system. Not the least of the ideas presented here is Dos Passos's conviction that the modern world enslaves man and defeats individualism of any kind.

Malcolm Cowley has pointed out that Dos Passos was, during his most productive years, two novelists: a realist and collectivist producing radical histories of the class struggle, and a late-Romantic aesthete unconcerned about social issues. As a member of the so-called "Harvard esthetes," he and his colleagues read and admired Walter Pater and assiduously separated their poetry from the reality of life and social conditions. The Harvard group was part of a larger movement, encompassing the writers who contributed to the Dial and earlier to The Yellow Book. Out of such an atmosphere developed the art novel, in which there are two central characters, the artist (protagonist) and the world (antagonist); the

115

typical conclusion of the struggle between the two is the defeat of
the artist's individuality.[2]

In *One Man's Initiation,* both elements are at work. Martin Howe
is the first of a long line of earnest young men who think their own
thoughts, try to live as individuals, and suffer defeat at the hands of
a crass world. But here the world is represented primarily by war,
and the novel ultimately becomes a denunciation of militarism. Although the author has not developed his keen interest in the plight
of men of all classes, so significant to the later works, lurking in the
background are adumbrations of most of the major ideas which are
to concern him as a collectivist. Dos Passos himself says of the
dichotomy of purpose, "I happen to be a journalist who's also interested in the art of writing, experimental methods, etc. I don't think
it's exactly a dichotomy because, for better or worse, my produc-
tions result from the interweaving of both impulses. After all
critics have to have their fun."[3] Both motives are, to some degree,
present in the work of most dedicated novelists of any society,
Fielding, Flaubert, Dostoievski, and Balzac, to name only a few.
It would appear that, as Dos Passos suggests, the critics have overemphasized the contrast in his novels. Perhaps it is more credible
to recognize the romantic impulse as a catalyst which shapes the
realistic material than to attempt assigning each novel to one
category or the other.

Understanding the technique of *One Man's Initiation* depends
upon an examination of the method whereby ideas are conveyed
to the reader, of the introduction of characters and theme that are
to become standard for most of Dos Passos's novels, and of the use
of innovations in language and symbolism. Such an analysis reveals
in a germinal stage most of the devices which make him unique and
significant in the history of the modern novel.

One of the most marked distinctions between the technique of
One Man's Initiation and succeeding novels is Dos Passos's method
of introducing social criticism. In *Manhattan Transfer* and *U.S.A.,*
his novels which are closest to being purely proletarian, he displays
an amazing degree of objectivity, a quality developed through
practice and experiment, that lifts him far above novelists such as
Upton Sinclair who cannot disguise the protest in the trappings of
their fiction. Here, Dos Passos is already motivated by the desire to
root out and correct injustices, but he has not yet learned the value

of the implied protest. Thus, the reader is informed pointedly that the author is a critic of capitalism and war. There are repeated polemics on socialism, communism, the church, and the relationship between the intellectual and the laborer, all rather awkwardly introduced through the medium of long argumentative conversations. Typical is the crucial chapter in which Martin and Tom Randolph talk with a group of French intellectuals. Dos Passos, in a preface to the 1945 edition (entitled *First Encounter*), singled out the chapter as an attempt to express the yearning that many young Americans felt during the war years to denounce capitalism and turn to communism. "As an American unaccustomed to the carefully articulated systems of thought which in those days were still part of the heritage of the European mind, I remember being amazed and delighted to meet men who could formulate their moral attitudes, Catholic, Anarchist, Communist, so elegantly."[4] The chapter contains a straightforward presentation of the protest that is the theme of this novel as well as of *Three Soldiers*. When a Frenchman inquires of Martin whether or not Americans like the war, Martin answers,

"They don't know what it is. They are like children. They believe in everything they are told, you see; they have had no experience in international affairs, like you Europeans. To me our entrance into the war is a tragedy."
"It's sort of going back on our only excuse for existin'," put in Randolph (*OMI*, 112–13).

The author is terrified by the ease with which man's mind may be enslaved, by the gullible acceptance of propaganda, by the use of flags and parades and appeals to patriotism to effect the "gradual unbaring of teeth" (*OMI*, p. 114). One of the French soldiers suggests that communism is the solution for the world's problems; another asserts that the answer lies within the Church, but he is contradicted by his comrades who insist that they themselves must throw off the bonds and form a new world. Similar ideas are presented in *U.S.A.*, but the author has learned by then to weave them carefully into the fabric of the narrative.

Stylistically, the first novel is unimpressive to a contemporary reader, though in places it foreshadows the lyric beauty and intensity of *Three Soldiers*. There are strikingly beautiful images and metaphors ("Intemperate desires prowled like cats in the darkness"), but the best expression of the poet Dos Passos is his use of impressionism in such passages as the following:

Dawn in a wilderness of jagged stumps and ploughed earth; against the yellow sky, the yellow glare of guns that squat like toads in a tangle of wire and piles of brass shellcases and split wooden boxes. Long rutted roads littered with shellcases stretching through the wrecked woods in the yellow light; strung along of them, tangled masses of telephone wires. Torn camouflage fluttering greenish-grey against the ardent yellow sky, and twining among the fantastic black leafless trees, the greenish wraiths of gas (*OMI*, 60, 81–82).

Here merely outpourings of the author's aestheticism, such strings of sense impressions will be used in *Manhattan Transfer* to convey the multifaceted life of the city. Later, the poetic urge will produce the terse, ironic biographies and the Camera Eye in the great trilogy.

An important language device in *One Man's Initiation* is juxta-position. Passages written in the present tense are interspersed with the conventional past tense narrative to dramatize the action, to infuse life and immediacy into the incident. Scenes diametrically opposed in tone and mood are introduced one after the other to produce the same effect of shock or surprise Dos Passos later achieves in the peculiar mixture of the serious and the maudlin in his Newsreels. One scene concludes with the pathetic lament of a young American soldier:

"There's nothing they can do against this new gas. . . . It just corrodes the lungs as if they were rotten in a dead body. In the hospitals they just stand the poor devils up against a wall and let them die. They say their skin turns green and that it takes from five to seven days to die—five to seven days of slow choking."

With no transitional material and only a space to separate the passages, another speaker is introduced, an American girl, come over to "do my bit" in the war effort: " 'Oh, but I think it's so splendid of you'—she bared all her teeth, white and regular as those in a dentist's show-case, in a smile as she spoke—'to come over this way to help France' " (*OMI*, 12–13). Without comment, the author conveys the irony inherent in the reality of war as opposed to its romanticized existence as a crusade to save democracy.

Irony, very much a part of the Dos Passos method, is introduced in other ways. Martin, sitting at a sidewalk cafe, enjoying "the musty scene of Paris, that mingled with the melting freshness of the wild strawberries on the plate before him," observes a French soldier who wears a patch on his face because his nose and jaw have been destroyed by a bullet or shell. The implication is that for many victims of war, the musty smell of Paris, the taste of straw-berries, and other simple pleasures of life are ended. Sometimes the irony is bitterly humorous, as in the portrayal of the French soldier committed to a psychiatric ward after going berserk: "He's crazy. He says that to stop the war you must kill everybody, kill everybody" (*OMI*, 40). Tom Randolph, after a night with a French girl he cannot praise highly enough ("My girl was charm-ing. . . . Honestly, I'd marry her in a minute"), tells his friend that he must go to the hotel for "preventitives." One ironic word shat-ters the illusion of love and exposes the typical American soldier's attitude toward the women of the country he has come to save.

The reader familiar with Dos Passos will recognize in the novel characters who are standard in most of his work. There is the art-novel hero, noted above, defeated in his struggle with the un-sympathetic world. Of this type Dos Passos says in the introduction to *First Encounter*: "I think the brutalities of war and oppression came as less of a shock to people who grew up in the thirties than they did to Americans of my generation, raised as we were during the quiet afterglow of the nineteenth century, among comfortably situated people who were confident that industrial progress meant an improved civilization, more of the good things of life all around, more freedom, a more humane and peaceful society" (*FE*, 7).

One Man's Initiation takes its title from Martin's expressed desire "to be initiated in all the circles of hell" (*OMI*, 69). Martin loses his faith in the war, then in social reform after his French friends are killed. Thus the message here is, in embryonic form, the same as that of several later novels: the man of sensibilities and aesthetic feelings must always be disillusioned in face of the present condi-tion of the world.

Another Dos Passos method which has its inception in this novel is the use of anonymous characters who offer a sort of choral com-ment on the action. In one scene, two unidentified soldiers discuss the war and Paris.

"They tell me that Paris is some city."

"The most immoral place in the world, before the war. Why, there are houses there where . . ." his voice sank into a whisper. The other man burst into loud guffaws.

"But the war's put an end to all that. They tell me that French people are regenerated, positively regenerated."

"They say the lack of food's something awful, that you can't get a square meal. They even eat horse."

"Did you hear what those fellows were saying about that new gas? Sounds frightful, don't it? I don't care a thing about bullets, but that kind o' gives me cold feet. . . . I don't give a damn about bullets, but that gas. . ." (*OMI*, 15).

Such dramatizations of the moods and feelings of an entire army in the person of one or two unnamed representatives are early indications of Dos Passos's development as a proletarian novelist.

The symbolism of *One Man's Initiation* is a practice run for the involved chain of symbols in *Three Soldiers*. There are the same songs and patriotic slogans; and some of the major symbols in the two books, as well as the messages they convey about war, are almost identical. In both instances, Dos Passos uses the herd image and the related idea of man's enslavement to the machine of militarism. In *One Man's Initiation*, Martin and an unidentified French soldier converse:

"Have you ever seen a herd of cattle being driven to an abattoir on a fine May morning?" asked the aspirant in a scornful, jaunty tone. . . .

"I wonder what they think of it."

"It's not that I'm resigned. . . . Don't think that. Resignation is too easy. That's why the herd can be driven by a boy of six . . . or a prime minister!" (*OMI*, 69).

Later Merrier, a Communist, argues that men "are too like sheep; we must go in flocks, and a flock to live must organize." His comrade Lully counters with the assertion that "you and I and our American friends are not sheep. We are capable of standing alone, of judging all for ourselves . . ." (*OMI*, 117–18). Discussing the social revolution they believe to be imminent after the war, Martin's French friends dream of a golden age in which a man will be free to live as he chooses, unencumbered by the ownership of property, unoppresed by other owners of property. But there is a more present danger, more deadly than capitalism: "'Of all slaveries, the slavery of war, of armies, is the bitterest, the most hopeless slavery.' Lully was speaking, his smooth brown face in a grimace of excitement and loathing. 'War is our first enemy'" (*OMI*, 123). In *Three Soldiers,* John Andrews develops this theme in a musical work dedicated to John Brown and the freedom of all mankind.

Another symbol common to the two novels is that of the *tabula rasa.* Martin, lying on the deck of the troop ship, dreams:

The future is nothing to him, the past is nothing to him. All his life is effaced in the grey languor of the sea, in the soft surge of the water about the ship's bow. . . . As through infinite mists of greyness he looks back on the sharp hatreds and wringing desires of his life. Now a leaf seems to have been turned and a new white page spread before him, clean and unwritten on. At last things have come to pass (*OMI*, 11).

To Martin, the bitter truth inevitably comes; like his creator, he comes to recognize the pointlessness of war, even of life in the modern world. The idea of the *tabula rasa,* Dos Passos says, had its origin in the faith with which his generation faced the world after the war, that "sanguine feeling that the future was a blank page to write on, focusing first about the speeches of Woodrow Wilson and then about the figure of Lenin . . ." (*FE,* 9). Already in the early twenties, the author had come to believe that war was of no value in sweeping aside the evils of the past, that, indeed, it only served to complicate the servitude of man in the modern world.

The contrast of past and present, represented by the destruction of cathedrals, is employed in the novel as a means of achieving unity. For Martin, the cathedral comes to symbolize the magnificence of the past; like Henry Adams, he recognizes something in the Middle Ages which gave to life and death a significance lacking in the modern world. In that quiet contented age, "the crude agony of life was seen through a dawnlike mist of gentle beauty." Martin yearns for such a refuge:

"God! if there were somewhere nowadays where you could flee from all this stupidity, from all this cant of governments, and this hideous reiteration of hatred, this strangling hatred . . . ," he would say to himself, and see himself working in the fields, copying parchments in quaint letterings, drowsing his feverish desires to calm in the deep-throated passionate chanting of the endless offices of the Church (*OMI*, 44).

A marked contrast to the quiet rhythm of the lives of the long-dead monks is the ragtime music played on the cathedral organ by Tom Randolph, music which resounds "like mocking laughter in the old vaults and arches" (*OMI*, 44). Shortly thereafter, the cathedral is bombed, and even Randolph is appalled by the destruction.[5]

War is further symbolized as a giant crap game with each bombardment representing a throw of the dice. On the troop ship bound for France, soldiers gather in a corner of the deck to shoot crap; later, lying in a dugout near the battlefield,

Howe saw the woods as a gambling table on which, throw after throw, scattered the random dice of death. . . . What right had a nasty little piece of tinware to go tearing through his rich, feeling flesh, extinguishing it? . . . Like dice thrown on a table, shells burst about the dugout, now one side, now the other. . . .

The casting of the dice began again, farther away this time.

"We won that throw," thought Martin (*OMI*, 105–106).

On another occasion, the protagonist thinks of the bombardment as a game of battledore and shuttlecock, "these huge masses whirling through the evening far above his head, now from one side, now from the other" (*OMI*, 32). War is as pointless as a game; and after a while, surrounded by the dead and the wounded, Martin comes to feel that war's stakes are no more important. Life itself becomes meaningless in the face of such wholesale slaughter.

The most significant type of symbol in the novel is the representative act, usually employed in bringing some significant idea into the narrative. Brief as it is, *One Man's Initiation* might be said to be a chain of such acts with very little transitional material between. Already Dos Passos has learned to move abruptly from one scene to another without many of the encumbrances of the traditional novel. An examination of two of the symbolic acts will serve to illustrate the form and purpose of this device. In one scene, a German prisoner in a labor battalion is critically injured by a barrage from his countrymen's guns. Martin, carrying the unfortunate man toward the hospital, feels suddenly peaceful, just as he did when he dreamed of being in a monastery.

The effort gave Martin a strange contentment. It was as if his body were taking part in the agony of this man's body. At last they were washed out, all the hatreds, all the lies, in blood and sweat. Nothing was left but the quiet friendliness of beings alike in every part, eternally alike (*OMI*, 104).

In this scene, which is essentially the turning point of the novel, Martin, like later Dos Passos protagonists, recognizes the brotherhood of men, the pointlessness of hatred and slaughter in the name of some governmental system. Another symbolic act, one of the concluding incidents of the plot, involves the meeting between Martin and a Frenchman who makes shoe laces from the boots of dead soldiers. Gathered about the man are "piles of old boots, rotten with wear and mud, holding fantastically the imprints of the toes and ankle-bones of the feet that had worn them." In the candlelight, they appear to move like the feet of wounded men in a dressing-station. Explaining his profession, the maker of shoe laces comments laconically on the irony of life and death: "Yes, many a good copain of mine has had his poor feet in those boots. What of it? Some day another fellow will be making laces out of mine, eh?" The scene comments effectively, if a bit too obviously, on the speed with which the machinery of war seizes, grinds up, and obliterates the lives of men.

Upon these symbolic acts rests the burden of the author's message; they represent the brutality of war, the paradoxes of life, the bitter aspects of existence. They are, furthermore, important steps in the initiation of Martin Howe into the circles of hell; they display his recognition that a man is a man, whether he be French, American, English, or German, and that in death if not in life, all are equal.

In the framework of such symbols, archetypal characters, and unassuming innovations in structure, Dos Passos developed his first novel. It is doubtful if any of the early readers of the volume imagined that the author was to become one of the geniuses of the twentieth-century novel. But inferior as it is in many respects, the novel is important as an illustration of the development of the author's technique. The use of the continuing symbol, introduced here, is later to be the foundation for *Three Soldiers* and *Manhattan Transfer*. And the symbolic act, perhaps the most significant aspect of *One Man's Initiation*, will subsequently be improved and employed as an effective instrument by the proletarian novelist. Dos Passos's first novel is an apprentice job; but as such, it is an important milestone in the history of his increasing powers as a technician.

DOROTHY BRATSAS

EXOTICISM IN THE PROSE OF
THE MEXICAN MODERNISTS

IN MEXICO, as in the rest of Spanish America, a number of different literary currents influenced the writers of the last two decades of the nineteenth century. For example, a persistent Romanticism was evident in the works of the Realists. Different writers praised or damned the Naturalist method. The poetically inclined were attracted by the French Parnassians and Symbolists. The polemics and literary experiments of the period reflected all of these influences. However, the Mexican literary experimenters sought primarily a new expression that would be fresher and more artistic than the generally imitative literature of earlier years. In their eagerness to move beyond the vulgarity of a materialistic society, the young writers were particularly attracted by Symbolism and Parnassianism. The *modernista* movement grew out of this need, with Manuel Gutiérrez Nájera as the pre-eminent initiator in Mexico.

Artistic discontent was expressed in a creative explosion which produced literary works of every conceivable type. Literary journals were the common meeting ground for the artists, and during this period many were founded with the express purpose of presenting works in a new idiom: *Revista Azul, Revista Moderna,* and *El Mundo Ilustrado* of Mexico; *El Cojo Ilustrado* of Venezuela; *Pluma y Lápiz* of Chile; and others. A common bond, the desire for freedom in artistic expression and development, united the young writers who contributed to and supported these publications. They did not call themselves *modernistas* nor did they strictly adhere to a specific set of artistic rules that would set them apart from their contemporaries. They were dissatisfied with the literature of preceding generations and wanted only to express themselves in a new fashion, representative of their interests, their artistic ideas, and their generation.

The aesthetic position maintained by the Modernist poets was in direct opposition to the materialistic society in which they lived and worked. A materialistic philosophy in which every aspect of human endeavor was evaluated and judged on a utilitarian basis was unacceptable to them. Consequently, the authors' emotional and intellectual reactions to their society were reflected in their non-fiction, in their prose fiction, and in their poetry.

The *modernistas* deplored the overemphasis on technology and the de-emphasis of the arts, as well as the attempt, as in Naturalism, to apply some of the prevailing scientific theories of the period to literature. They wanted to create an "art for art's sake."

An author's sensitivity to his period is often reflected in the vocabulary he uses in his works. The vocabulary of the Mexican *modernistas* reveals vividly the effects their social, educational, political, and artistic environment had upon them. They liked to use words from specialized vocabularies which were traditionally associated with various scientific disciplines, as well as with art. They created new and exciting images in order to show the existing relationships between seemingly unrelated things. Perfection of form was of paramount importance; and the Modernists strove for startling, sculptured, jewel-like images in their poetry. Landscape, architecture, *objets d'art,* foreign lands—anything exotic or having exotic connotations attracted their attention; and their imagery usually reflected the cosmopolitan quality of their interests. The prose fiction of the Mexican Modernists shows, too, the influence of their education and environment, an influence so strong that they employed some of the machinery furnished by the society they criticized and from which they wanted to escape.

The objective of this study is to examine one aspect of Mexican Modernism as it is reflected in the prose fiction of a generation of authors who were the major contributors to the *Revista Moderna.* For the sake of brevity and unity, only the short story and the novel will be examined; the *crónica* and *ensayo* are omitted. The principal years covered are those between 1894 and 1910: the majority of the pertinent works were written during this period. Some, however, principally those by Nervo, Rebolledo, and Tablada, were published as late as 1924. An extensive study has been made of the literary works of Amado Nervo, who is considered the major figure in Mexican Modernism; but little effort has been expended in the examination of the works of the lesser known authors: Efrén Rebolledo, Ernesto Leduc, Ciro B. Ceballos, Jesús E. Valenzuela, Carlos Díaz Dufóo, J. J. Tablada, and Bernardo Couto Castillo, the founder of the *Revista Moderna*.

The majority of these writers at one time or another had the opportunity to travel beyond the national boundaries of their country. Their peripatetic adventures led them to countries as diverse as Japan and Norway or Italy and Denmark. When a young writer was not fortunate enough to be of independent means or successful in securing a diplomatic appointment, like Nervo, he sought other means of achieving his goal—he sought a sponsor. It was due to the largesse of such a sponsor, the *Revista Moderna*, that J. J. Tablada was able to make his journey to Japan. The fruits of his travels appeared in the many articles he contributed to the journal: fifteen appeared between April, 1900, and March, 1901, on subjects as disparate as a Japanese Noh play and the funeral of an important Japanese official. It was also in 1900 that the *Revista Moderna* sponsored Amado Nervo's trip to France. The glamor and exoticism that one associates with foreign and distant lands wove a spell over them. Some, like Nervo and Efrén Rebolledo, spent part of their most productive years in foreign lands as diplomatic representatives of Mexico; and some died, as Nervo did in Montevideo, far from their native country.

The degree of exoticism in the work of the *modernistas* varied. The exotic quality or atmosphere was enhanced by placing the tales in a foreign country; by selecting protagonists from Greek or Norse mythology, fairy tales, and folk lore; or by introducing an established fictional character from another genre into Mexican literature. A case in point is Pierrot, a French character utilized by Couto Castillo in a series of tales. This clown protagonist had been created by drama in the eighteenth century and had been perpetuated through the years not only in the theater but also in prose fiction.

Pierrot was a leading character in French pantomime plays; in the theater, he was traditionally costumed in clown's garb and was presented as an extremely capricious, erratic, and eccentric personality. During the nineteenth century this character was incorporated into prose as well as poetry, appearing in the works of Gautier, de Banville, and Catulle Mendès. A transformation occurred in Pierrot, however, when prose writers borrowed him from the theater: he became a sad, melancholy, pathetic, and romantic figure. There were variations on his presentation, but the major difference was his melancholia. In the works of Couto Castillo he was still as capricious and unpredictable as he was in eighteenth-century theater, but there appeared an undercurrent of sensitivity that varied in intensity from story to story.

In Couto Castillo's five stories various facets of Pierrot's personality are presented. In "Pierrot y sus gatos" he wanders about the streets of Paris venting his Baudelairean *spleen.* In "Las nupcias de Pierrot," Pierrot has changed from the cynical and independent Baudelairean young man to a Mallarméan youth in search of his ideal. Pierrot travels deep into the forest, becomes tired, and falls asleep. As he dreams, he sheds his mask of cynicism and irony; and the mocker becomes sensitive and compassionate. He has a desire to love and be loved and sets out in search of his Colombina. Instead of being in the forest, he finds himself in a beautiful garden populated by fauns and nymphs, containing statues of muses, goddesses, Bacchus, tritons, and sirens spouting water from their marble mouths. Then, Pierrot awakens at sunset and sees before him two beautiful women. They are sisters, one named Locura and the other Ideal. Locura offers her sister to Pierrot. By accepting Ideal's hand in marriage, Pierrot would achieve the happiness and peace that he has longed for. The melancholy sister, Locura, tells him that she had been tempted many times in the past to kiss him but that she had decided against it. Rather than give him madness, she preferred to give him peace, security, and happiness. When she leaves, Pierrot becomes aware of a nebulous figure in the background and recognizes Death. But all his former anxieties, fears, or apprehensions about Death are no longer of consequence. Because he has found his bride, Ideal, he can withstand any challenge or tribulation without fear.

This story parallels in many respects Mallarmé's *L'après-midi d'un faune* . In each of the two works, written in different languages and different mediums, the authors deal with the real and the imaginary. As in the story about Pierrot, when the Faun awakens from a dream which had been populated with nymphs, he is not sure that he has been dreaming. The intermingling of dream and reality is characteristic of the poem as well as the short story. Both protagonists are in a state of suspension as they contemplate the problem of reality and after moments of reflection decide that they have been dreaming:

> These nymphs I would perpetuate.
>   So clear
> Their light carnation, that it floats in the air
> Heavy with tufted slumbers.
>   Was it a dream I loved?
> My doubt, a heap of ancient night, is finishing
> In many a subtle branch, which, left the true
> Wood itself, proves, alas! that all alone I gave
> Myself for triumph the ideal sin of roses.[1]

After raising his hand to his forehead in an unsuccessful attempt to remember, he made a gesture of resignation and melancholia when he realized that he was embracing a rose. He felt satiated, disembodied, apathetic, and bewildered. He plucked the rose and inhaled its fragrance as he gently held it captive in his hands. He lay there, immobile, gazing into the distance and breathing with satisfaction. Only the perfume and a fleeting vision of the landscape remained from his dream.[2]

As in Mallarmé's poem, Pierrot encounters the two sisters. The Faun's dark and cruel nymph is equivalent to Pierrot's Locura and the blond, gentle, and naïve nymph to Ideal. The poem is a masterpiece of ambiguity in which the real or imagined presence of the nymphs tantalizes the Faun. He lives in a tenuous world; it is difficult for him to distinguish what is or is not a dream. The one reality that he has is his music and his pipes. Through his art he evokes and creates his realities. The works parallel each other through the introduction of the sisters, but from this point they cease to resemble each other in plot. They do, however, exploit the same theme. With his pipes the Faun creates his art, evokes his dreams, and dispels his fears. Pierrot likewise finds his ideal, his illusion in the young girl, and he is secure. Moreover, although the protagonists of the two works are dissimilar—the animalistic vitalism of the young satyr versus the melancholia of Pierrot—the works resemble each other strongly in mood and atmosphere.

Paris is the setting for the last three Pierrot stories,[3] and the reader is never permitted to forget its exoticism. That glamorous and ancient city lends itself well to the variable moods of the protagonist. Melancholia is the pervading one in all of the stories. However, Pierrot has not stated in his previous appearances what the factors are that have produced his melancholia. Finally, in the last Pierrot tale he expresses himself rather eloquently on his reasons for having felt disillusioned. Pierrot says that since the death of Gautier and De Banville, he has been neglected and forgotten. The world has become too involved in commerce and in making money and has become too conservative. Conservatism is reflected in the actions and the dress of the people, as well as in their language. Beauty has been fast disappearing from a world which has converted itself into a bank.[4] Even his Colombina has eloped with a banker. Therefore, he rejects society and its cult of the material and superficial; he goes to live in a cemetery. He finds peace and happiness in tending the graves and caring for the flowers, as well as in burying the insensitive bourgeois. At night he and his dead friends, who leave their graves, congregate and entertain each other with delightful parties. The bourgeois, the usurers, and the people who during their lifetime were concerned with the material are excluded from the parties and are not permitted to leave their graves. Only the dreamers, the poets, the artists, and the many people society considers lazy and useless because of their nonmaterial interests are permitted to attend the social gatherings. Pierrot says that he has withdrawn from the world forever and will not return because the conditions that exist are abhorrent to him.

The Pierrot who was described in the previous tales is more than a capricious, quixotic, and perverse *boulevardier*. He is a tragic figure in search of his identity, his lost image. The grimace which he wears like a badge is always worn for the benefit of society and is never removed. Only in his sleep and in his dreams does the mask disappear and reveal the sensitive artist in search of his ideal. Pierrot is a crepuscular and nocturnal creature who dares not face the merciless noonday sun. His damning of established institutions,

such as the belief in God, and his cultivation of the perverse
though lyrical invocation of Satan are his revenge, his rejection of
a society which he considers crude and insensitive to beauty, his
ideal. So, in the final story, he declares that he will never return to
the world but will devote himself to his unworldly activities. He
elects to live the remainder of his life in the marmoreal splendor of
his cemetery far removed from the superficialities of a daily existence devoted to the never ending pursuit of the material, removed
from a world so obsessed with the commercial that beauty in
language, dress, living, and the arts have been neglected and are
fast being forgotten. The Baudelairean Pierrot, confused and
caught within the complexities of urban living, the Pierrot who had
searched and in his search had subjected himself to some perverse
experiences, rejects the material world and descends into the unreal
Mallarméan Nirvana of his cemetery. He divorces himself forever
from society and lives in a world of illusion, where only an artist can
find complete happiness.

These stories are less important stylistically than they are
thematically. However, there is the noticeable use of a significant
linguistic device. It is embodied in the intriguing adjective, *abra-
cadabrantemente,* which Couto Castillo uses to describe the musi-
cianship of Pierrot. Using words that one usually associates with
children or childhood and transforming them into an adjective, ad-
verb, or verb is refreshing and exciting. Rimbaud was a past master
in utilizing this technique, especially notable in "Le Bateau Ivre,"
"Ma Bohème," and "Roman." The following is an example of this
literary device: "Comme je descendais des Fleuves impassibles, / Je
ne me sentis plus guidé par les haleurs: / Des Peaux-Rouges criards
les avaient pris pour cibles, / Les ayant cloués nus aux poteaux de
couleurs."[5] Thus, a unique and new frame of reference is revealed
to the artist as well as to the reader. The artist's horizon of expression has been expanded and a whole new set of relationships has
been presented to him. The writer's movement and expression have
become less restricted. In the same way, these young authors, the
Modernists, were seeking freedom, less restraint, and less regimenta-
tion of their creative efforts. In an attempt to revitalize the language,
they tried to show the relationships between apparently contradic-
tory or unrelated experiences. This was not an original stylistic
device; it had been employed earlier by the French. After the pub-

lication of Baudelaire's poem, "Correspondances," many post-Baudelairean poets like Rimbaud, Mallarmé, Lautréamont, and Laforgue worked diligently in employing his theory of *correspondances* in an attempt to expand their artistic horizon. The French use of such correspondences inspired Couto Castillo to attempt some of these techniques in Spanish. It is tragic that he died so young, for it would have been interesting to see his development. He showed marked ability and ingenuity. He was gifted in evoking subtle feelings as well as delicacy of expression. His ability to create a feeling of nebulousness, intangibility, and the illusory imbued his work with a dreamlike quality that is especially obvious in the Pierrot stories. The subject matter lent itself handsomely to this desired effect, though the result was not always successful.

The desire to escape from reality and to travel and dwell in an imaginary and exotic world is not solely the province of one age-group. It is appealing to all. The make-believe world of a child juxtaposes the grotesque and the beautiful. It is a fantastic region brilliantly colored and heavily populated with giants, dwarfs, witches, fairies, dragons, steeds, handsome gallants, and beautiful damsels. At the slightest wish the laws of nature may be suspended while cows jump over the moon and coaches turn into pumpkins. The adult world has its make-believe land, but it is peopled with its own special goblins and fairies who have more sophisticated tastes. Its witches are transformed into Medusas, its giants into Cyclopes, its dragons into Cerberuses, its knights into satyrs, and its maidens into nymphs. Ceballos takes his reader into such a world in his story "El viejo fauno." For many years an old satyr has been kidnapping young nymphs and taking them to his lair. Because they always die there, he is forced to abduct a new girl each spring. Astarte becomes quite displeased especially when he kidnaps another nymph. In order to punish him, Astarte turns the nymph into a golden skeleton. Neither the plot nor all of the images and figures of speech are startlingly original. However, Ceballos was trying to be original in technique and create an aura of pastoral splendor and elegance. At times he almost achieves a marmorean quality in his prose. He uses synesthesia in this story, for example, in the following descriptions: the shade of the dead nymph is "un esqueleto de oro de musicales vértibras," and the new nymph is "un sensitivo cuerpo sensitivo y balsámico."[6]

Only one story by the *modernistas* utilizes the Indian folk lore of Mexico. The story, by J. J. Tablada, is called "El dios de Netzahualcoyotl."[7] It is a retelling of the Aztec legend of the king whose lost empire was reconquered by his son. The story is told in a straightforward and unembellished manner, accompanied by beautiful illustrations taken from the original manuscript Tablada used to make his translation. It is unfortunate that these young authors did not see fit to use the pre-Columbian culture of their country in their literary endeavors. Only in the years after World War I has a tremendous interest been generated in the indigenous cultures of Mexico.

There is one tale by Díaz Dufóo in which he describes the first slave in the world.[8] The story is an account of the life and activities of a primitive couple in India. Their tribe has been involved in a fight for survival with neighboring tribes. No prisoners are ever taken because there is not enough food for them. The couple's tribe is nomadic, their religion devoted to worship of a Fire God. This tribe has heard vague rumors about another tribe which cultivates land, but they have no knowledge of them. Sakya and his mate, Varuni, are captured by this more advanced tribe. The two are not killed but are made slaves and forced to till the land. Thus, Sakya becomes the first slave and weeps bitterly for his lost freedom. The story is written objectively, without authorial intrusion. Yet there is a lyrical quality that at times sings forth from the prose. The following words are typical of the vocabulary the author uses to give the story fluidity and lyrical quality: *plateadas, ígnea, fiera, rojizo crepúsculo,* and *antorcha.* Díaz Dufóo uses simple uncomplicated constructions which are not in the least labored or forced. The following is an example of his style in this story: "Vapor de fuego se eleva de las charcas: en los aires el ave de rapiña grazna ferozmente al descubrir su presa. La serpiente se arrastra en ondulaciones vagas." [A hot mist rises up from the pools: in the air a plundering bird caws ferociously upon discovering its prey. The serpent drags itself about in vague circles.][9]

"Exempli Gratia"[10] is the opposite of the preceding tale. Rather than primitive India, the setting is Turin, Italy, during the Middle Ages. The story concerns seven troubadours who have gone to sing at a castle. After entertaining for a while, they decide to leave because of the drunkenness and debauchery. Just as they are leaving a heavenly fire strikes the castle and everyone dies. Everyone is turned to ashes except the troubadours; they are turned to stone and thus immortalized so that centuries later they can be seen by everyone.

The stylistic differences between the two stories are due to the differences in subject matter. In his story Díaz Dufóo described a primitive culture whereas Tablada described the wealth and richness of the life of the Middle Ages. Tablada intrudes at the beginning of the story to tell his reader that he was inspired to write it after having seen a Gobelin tapestry. He begs his reader's indulgence and then begins to tell his story. Tablada's interest in art extended to all ages and cultures, Eastern as well as Western. The source of his inspiration accounts for the use of words rich in color, texture, vibrancy, and brilliance; they give a tapestry effect to his story. He also describes and names the musical instruments used by the troubadours: *laúd, con crótalo, el místico theorbe, el rabel,* and uses words associated with the Middle Ages like *glauca, melena, hamadríade, halconero, landagraviata, pucela,* and *adamantina.* There is no character development in the work; that is not its purpose. The author is interested in creating an effect, a word tapestry in which the movement of the protagonists is controlled and two-dimensional, static rather than fluid.

These writers had a desire for knowledge and experience that took them to all parts of the world. Because of their cosmopolitanism they were interested in describing the environment, the customs, or the cultures of the lands they visited. They made no attempt to develop or express any philosophical concept. Rebolledo and Tablada had the opportunity to travel extensively, especially in the Orient. Both spent a considerable length of time in Japan, although at different intervals.[11] They both wrote articles or stories making use of their travel experiences. A great many nonfictional works by Tablada, describing his experiences in Japan, appeared in the *Revista Moderna;* but only one short story utilizes a Japanese setting. Unfortunately, it is not outstanding. Its primary interest lies in the description of Japanese customs of death and mourning. The plot is a traditional one concerning the perfidy of woman.

Efrén Rebolledo wrote a novel, *Hojas de bambú,*[12] in which the majority of the action takes place in Japan. After the hero, Abel Morán, graduates from law school, his father gives him a considerable sum of money to be used as he wishes. His interest in the Orient, Japan in particular, has been excited by reading the works of Marco Polo, Edmond de Goncourt, Pierre Loti, and Lafcadio Hearn. He decides to use the gift to underwrite his trip to Japan. The remainder of the story concerns his adventures en route as well as on the return trip. The plot of the novel is trite and dull. The figures of speech and the images are most unoriginal. The only thing that may hold the reader's interest is the author's curiosity about Japan. The *name* of the country excites the imagination of the reader and creates or stimulates a feeling of exoticism; this alone may hold his interest, though with difficulty. The novel does offer some information: Geisha houses are not brothels; the only social event of importance for the diplomatic corps is the Japanese Imperial Garden Party.

Two novels of this movement appeared in the early twenties of this century, *Saga de Sigrida la blonda* by Efrén Rebolledo and *Resurrección de los ídolos* by J. J. Tablada. Compared with the other works already discussed, their publication was late. By 1919 the majority of the *modernista* prose works had been published. Actually the major works, the works of more literary merit, had appeared by 1910. The chaotic conditions resulting from the Revolution of 1910 seem to have had a strong effect upon the literary output of the movement. Except for the works of two writers who died before the outbreak of hostilities[13] and Amado Nervo, who was far removed from the scene in a diplomatic post in Madrid, for a time it produced no further products. The other writers became very much involved in the advancement of their respective nonliterary careers. Of the *modernista* works after 1910, many are by Nervo; and the remainder are by Efrén Rebolledo and J. J. Tablada, who began to write again in this tradition only after peace was reestablished. The Rebolledo work is an anachronism. The nation had been involved in a bitter social revolution for several years before the appearance of the novel. In spirit and style it parallelled the literary efforts of the late nineteenth century. The fascination with the foreign was still in evidence, but there was no attempt at an original presentation of material.

The novel, *Saga de Sigrida la blonda*,[14] is the story of a young Mexican diplomat who meets a Norwegian adolescent, Sigrida, and is extremely impressed with her delicate beauty. Three years later he meets her again in Switzerland. They fall in love, and their affair is continued in Norway, where Edmundo is stationed. Sigrida is quite enamored of Edmundo and readily agrees to marry him. Before they can marry, he is transferred to a new post in San Francisco. Although he is forced to leave without her, he promises to return. By the time he does, he finds that Sigrida has died, a suicide.

The novel has many flaws. The protagonists are wooden, unreal, and artificial. Everything about them seems contrived. In the development of Sigrida's character, no logical reason is advanced for her suicide. The author attempts to create an impressionistic atmosphere in his novel. In describing and developing Sigrida, he unsuccessfully attempts to create a Norse naiad in a setting of ice and the aurora borealis. The work is imaginatively barren. There is a monotonous repetition of the same words without any originality of expression: *blonda, rubia, azúl, tierna, santa, fría, helado,* and *hada.* The author likes to include in his work many references to Ibsen, Björnson, Grieg, and Norse mythology, as well as to Norwegian words and phrases. He also constantly refers to Poe and in several places actually paraphrases him: "Es una noche del helado octubre, en la fría Noruega, a orillas del fjord. Es una fría noche de octubre, como en el pavoroso poema de Ulalume." [It is a night in cold October, in frigid Norway, by the banks of a fjord. It is a night in cold October, as in the appalling poem, "Ulalume."][15] These references to Poe and others to Scandinavian authors are unsuccessfully incorporated into the body of the work and detract from rather than add to its artistic success. One is left with the impression of a travelogue of others' works as well as of Norway.

Tablada's *Resurrección de los ídolos*[16] presents a somewhat different problem. It is the only lengthy work devoted to the *Mexican* scene of that period. It deals with postrevolutionary Mexico and touches upon the *indianista* problems, as well as upon the conflict of good and evil within man. The subject matter of the novel places it in an entirely different literary category, but it is exotic in its descriptions of the pre-Cortesian cultures of Mexico. The novel abounds in local color: the setting is Xipe, and much of the action revolves around the Temazcale Indians and their culture.

None of the works of this movement can be considered exceptional or of outstanding literary merit. The authors were cosmopolitan because they were interested in the exotic. They were seeking out new lands, cultures, environments, both past and present, in order to enlarge their artistic horizon. Their exoticism reveals itself in various ways: the action and setting of the tale or novel occurs in a foreign country or mythological kingdom; or the protagonists are selected from folklore, mythology, or some other source, as was Pierrot in the Couto Castillo tales, and placed in new situations and predicaments by the authors. In some poorly written works the only saving grace is their setting, a country arousing the curiosity and interest of the reader. The majority of the works are uneven, and most are rather mediocre; but an interesting linguistic change occurs in them. There seems to be a conscious effort at revitalizing the language, breaking with established tradition, and finding new relationships between related or seemingly unrelated emotions, things, or objects, concrete or intangible. Quite often these relationships are strained, but at times they are very well-executed. For example, Tablada describes a newspaper's printed page as "tatuada como la piel de un salvaje."[17] These new comparisons enriched and enlarged the writers' vocabulary. The stylistic techniques, however, were used less in the *cuento* and the novel than in the *crónica* and the poetry by the same authors. The *modernistas* were experimentalists in search of a new means of expression. Their literary efforts introduced new and original comparisons and relationships which enriched and enlarged their individual artistic scope.

MARIE LAGARDE

CARMONTELLE:

Portraitist of an Era

A WRITER of small talent is frequently forgotten, misplaced, or lost among the great literary figures of an epoch. This is unfortunate, since by reason of the quantity and authenticity of detail which preserve the language, ideas, atmosphere, and manners of the time, the work of such a writer can be of inestimable value for persons interested in studying a particular period. This is true of Louis Carrogis, known as "Carmontelle" or "Carmontel" (1717–1806), who is almost totally eclipsed by his brilliant French contemporaries.

The double aspect of his work links Carmontelle to the history of art as well as to the history of the theater. However, today Carmontelle the portraitist and author of dramatic proverbs is known only to a few artists, some eighteenth-century literary specialists, and persons interested in artistic and literary oddities. As a *portraitiste à la gouache* Carmontelle has left a number of albums containing more than six hundred portraits which form a picture-gallery of the second half of the eighteenth century. As author of the *proverbes dramatiques* Carmontelle is less known than as an artist, but in that capacity he has left a wealth of material for persons interested in examining the society of the same period. His hundreds of *proverbes* form a document whose ampleness, scope, and accurate detail give it a singular importance. From the quantity of information which they contain, there emerges a picture which is curiously authentic, the image and soul of a society which disappeared with the Revolution.

In spite of his obscure origins as the son of a guild cobbler, Carmontelle succeeded in making himself indispensable to the amusement and pleasure of the elite of Paris. He was sought after by the great and near-great for his talents as poet, actor, painter, sculptor, master mason, pyrotechnic specialist, hydraulic engineer, impresario, stage designer, landscape gardener, as well as for his personal charm. The usually caustic Bachaumont states that Carmontelle not only succeeded in almost every enterprise he undertook, but that he managed to distinguish himself.[1] A contemporary gives an idea of Carmontelle's achievement in landscape gardening, for example, when he estimates that society would sooner have dispensed with the services of Le Nôtre during the reign of Louis XIV than with those of Carmontelle during the last decades of the eighteenth century.[2]

In 1763 Carmontelle became *lecteur* of the Duke of Chartres, eldest son of the Duke of Orleans and the future Philippe-Egalité, and was later made director of the festivities of the Duke of Orleans. These *fêtes* were numerous and magnificent since the Duke was owner of eight or more châteaux in the environs of Paris. In this almost royal atmosphere Carmontelle was to preside in particular over the organization of the *fêtes* of the court of the Duke himself, of Madame de Montesson whom the Duke married in 1773, of the Duke of Chartres, and of Mademoiselle, the eldest daughter of the Duke. In general, he was to contribute to the amusement of the best society of Paris until the Revolution.

The Baron de Frénilly, who knew Carmontelle during the years when the latter was *lecteur* of the Duke of Chartres, describes him as rather thin, with a long severe face and a laugh that was a bit sardonic. He was inclined to be haughty in manner, at times even irascible. However, for those who knew him, this forbidding exterior concealed a generous heart and a soul which was singularly noble. His pride was the greater because he knew he was poor; he contributed to the amusement of the nobility of France as a friend doing a favor: an artist who asked no fee for his skill and time, a gentleman who went about on foot because he could not afford a carriage. He possessed all the little social graces so necessary to his century, "the trifling century in which he lived."[3]

The Marquise de Genlis, niece by marriage of the Duke of Orleans, was a frequent visitor at the court of the Duke both in Paris and at Villers-Cotterets, his favorite residence. She writes that Carmontelle was a man of considerable learning, of gentle disposition, and of irreproachable moral character, the latter a unique compliment when one considers the society in which Carmontelle spent most of his life. People liked to converse with him and sought his approbation. He was obliging, possessed a quick intellect and a keen sense of observation, an unusual combination in the opinion of the Marquise. Carmontelle observed closely his fellow men, not from malice but from a desire to know and understand people. Madame de Genlis concludes by stating that to speak of Carmontelle's character, his conduct, his wit, was to praise him.[4]

Although he was sought after for his many and varied talents, it was as portraitist and as author of the *proverbes* that Carmontelle made himself indispensable. A modest and charming man, he produced dainty pastel drawings and within a few hours could sketch almost perfect likenesses of the Duke's guests. The albums, begun before 1763 and to which new sheets were added each day, give an idea of the men and women of all walks of life, from the Dauphin of France to the floor polisher of the château of Saint-Cloud. Without Carmontelle we would know nothing or at best very little of most of them. For the artist, making the pastels and the pen sketches was a pastime and not a livelihood. He made them as effortlessly as though he were playing a game, or as though he were taking notes on the society in which he spent most of his life. He refused to sell the portraits, preferring to keep them for himself; but from time to time he would make copies which he offered as gifts to persons whom he considered his special friends, as he did with those of Diderot, the Baron Grimm, and Madame du Deffand. Only after the Revolution, when he was in need of money, did Carmontelle consent to sell several of the gouaches; and then he was careful to sell them to acquaintances who he felt were devoted to him.[5]

In spite of his success as an artist Carmontelle's *genre de prédilection* remained the *proverbe dramatique*. Little or badly as he is known as a writer today, in the eighteenth century Carmontelle's name was synonymous with the dramatic proverb, as that of Theocritus was with the idyl, that of La Fontaine with the fable, or that of Beethoven with the sonata.[6] During the last decades of the century he was considered the master and the most prolific producer of the genre, one of the popular light literary forms. In 1767 the Baron Grimm wrote, "Carmontelle furnishes plays just as a pastry-cook furnishes pastry shells . . . he has them presented in all the social groups everywhere."[7] Few persons were aware that the dramatic proverb had existed before Carmontelle, and in the nineteenth century no less a critic than Sainte-Beuve refers to Carmontelle as *le créateur du genre*.[8]

In the words of Carmontelle, the *proverbe dramatique* was a sort of comedy whose purpose was to illustrate a well-known proverb. It could be based on an invented subject, on some character trait, on some little story or anecdote, or on some adventure.[9] In fact, a number of Carmontelle's *proverbes* are nothing more than the acting out of some incident, or accident, which had befallen a person or persons whom the spectators recognized without great difficulty. The memoirs and correspondence of the century furnish the details and permit one to name with certainty Carmontelle's sources and models. The *mot du proverbe*, the concealed proverb, was to be enveloped in the action. The more popular the proverb, the more removed from it must be the action of the comedy, since the appreciation of the *proverbe* depended upon the difficulty or facility with which the proverb was "discovered." The whole was to be so constructed that when told what the *mot* was, the spectator must exclaim and be surprised and disappointed that he had not discovered it for himself.[10] Carmontelle based the framework for these tableaux, for which he prepared the necessary décor, on an allusion or a word. He excelled in improvising dialogues as finely drawn as his sketches. The Baron de Frénilly notes that Carmontelle's imagination and resourcefulness were inexhaustible in everything which concerned the staging and production of the *proverbes*.[11]

Since they were intended for private theaters, the *théâtres de société*, the *proverbes dramatiques* comprise a repertory of comedies which were easy to learn and to perform, in which one could display as much, or as little, natural or acquired talent as he might possess without exposing himself to the ridicule of a public. Talent, natural wit, the habits, and even the tics of the actors could be incorporated into the action. Memory failures, inexperience, inequality in natural ability, lack of unity and harmony detracted little from the charm of such presentations.

During the years from 1760 to 1789, when Carmontelle was writing his *proverbes*, a veritable *théâtromanie* had taken possession of society, especially the upper classes. The make-believe world of the theater was the means par excellence of beguiling the boredom which seems to have invaded the soul of this insouciant and superficial society, from the royal family to the lowest ranks. According to one literary historian, this fancy, which had been popularized by certain princes and nobles, became "imperceptibly a passion, a universal rage, reaching into all ranks of society, to such a degree that this talent comprises to some extent an integral part of the education of the time, and at a given moment, one can count in Paris alone, one hundred and sixty private theaters."[12]

There was no prince or noble who did not have one or more theaters in which the noble would-be actors defied censorship when the occasion arose.[13] The Duke of Orleans had at least eight; the *robe* and *finance*, persons important in legal and financial circles, as well as men of letters, actresses, and actors, also had private theaters. Voltaire, for example, had two, while "la Guimard," a popular actress of the time, had several. According to their means members of the lesser bourgeoisie had theaters for their own use, and even the artisans were affected. One of them, a ladies' cobbler named Charpentier, established in his domicile a *théâtre de société* and himself played the rôle of Orosmane in Voltaire's *Zaïre*.[14] This theater seems to have been the rage, for even the Duke of Chartres attended in company with several lords of the Court. The Duke went to the performance in a coach drawn by six horses; but in spite of the splendid equipage and the magnificent retinue, he had difficulty procuring tickets for the burlesque presentation.[15] Regardless of the ridicul which Piron's *Métromanie* heaped on the bourgeois histrions, the example of the nobles and of the bourgeois of Paris was followed by would-be actors in the remotest provinces.[16]

More than likely Carmontelle took advantage of this mania to express his opinions on the excesses of the time and to depict society with a realism which even his contemporaries recognized.[17] Prepared by experience and endowed as he was, Carmontelle was well-qualified for the task of portraying the lives of the populace, the bourgeoisie, and the nobility. He had known the artisans in his father's shop; he had been aide-de-camp during the Seven Years' War; as director of the *fêtes* of the elite of Paris, he had seen the inside of the *grand monde*. At times the surprising sincerity of the *proverbes dramatiques* detracts from their literary value, but it is precisely that quality which gives them the authenticity which makes them valuable from a sociological point of view. They are replete with fragments which reveal the moral tenor and the libertine atmosphere of the century. These vignettes may be unadorned, but they are witty and based on nature, that is, eighteenth-century society as Carmontelle saw it.

There can be little doubt that Carmontelle knowingly wrote a satire of his time. He could not have been unaware that in reproducing exactly what he saw and heard, he was holding society up to ridicule. His contemporaries have commented on the fact that Carmontelle listened to people, that he remembered their conversations and then seemed to write as though he were taking dictation, permitting himself neither suppression nor addition, neither correction nor choice.[18] In this almost quasi-stenographic recording he renders with amazing fidelity the habits of thought and of speech, the vocabulary, the mannerisms, and that indefinable quality which differentiated the upper from the lower classes and which proclaims, in its ensemble, the social stratum of each speaker.[19] As a result, it is never a complicated literary contrivance which the author presents, but rather the nooks and corners, the ins and outs of eighteenth-century society: a conversation in a salon; a quarrel in a boudoir; an argument in a neighborhood shop; a meeting in a theater lobby, at the opera, in a café; a conversation in the Tuileries gardens where the people one meets are very different from those who frequent the garden of the Palais-Royal. Carmontelle gives us an opportunity to see the people of Paris in the places where they liked to gather. At times the scenes are caricatures, or bawdy; however, one is confident that Carmontelle has seen and heard what he reproduces.

Carmontelle was less interested in developing characters than in portraying social types with which he came into contact, and in this he was as skillful with his pen as he was with his brush. We see the man of fashion, the social parasite, the fop, the "frequenter of boudoirs and of theater wings," the lover; the jealous, the henpecked, the cuckolded husband; the *abbé galant,* the ambitious and mundane bishop, the simple and simple-minded curé, the garrulous country priest; the *nouveau-riche;* the noble, and the bourgeois lecher; the little shopkeeper, the greedy and grasping peasant; valet, crook, cardsharp; the socialite, the blue-stocking, the romantic; the chatterbox, the ambitious and scheming wife, the affected bourgeoise; the shopkeeper's wife, the avaricious peasant woman; the widow, satisfied and dissatisfied; the prostitute of the boulevards and the tart of the Halles, and so on almost ad infinitum. Each type is presented in a situation according to his station and expresses ideas and opinions in language suited to his class. In Carmontelle's generally realistic dialogues, one exception is evident: when the author attempts to reproduce a tender scene between lovers, the dialogue becomes colorless and dull; the author seems to be out of his element. After all, one was not likely to encounter such a scene in a crowded salon.

Apparently Carmontelle had no intention of exercising a moralizing influence on his contemporaries unless one considers the exact and often not-to-be-envied picture of the times an attempt to chastise. He plainly states his aim in the following words taken from the foreword of the least known of his works, the *Conversations des gens du monde dans tous les tems de l'année.*

The author feels obliged to warn those who read this work that they will find nothing new, and that he [the author] has only collected what he heard every day: the aim of the author is, therefore, not to instruct, but on the contrary, to teach foreigners how to speak without saying anything.[20]

Carmontelle wrote to enrich the pleasures of the society in which he lived; and if demand is taken as a measure of success, then he was successful. One would make an error, however, to misjudge the nature of Carmontelle's talent. Taking cognizance of the superficiality of the environment in which he lived and of the absurdities of the people around him, he could not fail to make use of the opportunity which such a society offered as material for the *proverbes dramatiques.* Although his censure, if one may wish to call it that, was in general not bad-tempered, Carmontelle could not restrain himself from casting stinging barbs from time to time. He showed impatience with the excesses of the time, with the selfish and absurd caprices of the nobility and the wealthy, with their mania for satisfying every whim, with the despotism of "fashion, that tyrant of reason,"[21] which dictated every action of one's life, even to the minutest detail.

Since Carmontelle seems not to have been the dupe of the conventions of his century, he was able to observe and appraise them in an objective manner. He saw the unconcern and fickleness of the idle and bored nobility, the vanity and ambition of the enriched bourgeoisie, the avarice and pettiness of the lower classes. He showed in relief the cruelty only too often concealed under the extravagant and brittle brilliance of the *grand monde,* exposing with pitiless accuracy and thoroughness the less presentable side of a world which had money and pleasure for its principal goals. He did so with a verve not found in the works of the great writers of the century. In depicting the *robe* and *finance,* Carmontelle frequently portrayed those individuals who were ambitious to contract alliances with the titled nobility, heedless of the consequences to family and self-respect. Less caustic where the lower bourgeoisie and the *peuple* are concerned, the author of the *proverbes dramatiques* seemed content to smile good-naturedly at the eccentricities and failings which made the subject ridiculous but which caused no harm to anyone else. It is this portrayal of all social classes which makes the *proverbes* a living tableau and a criticism of the mores of the last half of the eighteenth century.

After looking at the portraits and reading the *proverbes dramatiques,* one is strongly inclined to conclude that the two should not or perhaps cannot be separated. They constitute an ensemble of documents of a rare sincerity which, completing and supporting one another, provide a picture of contemporary society whose equal one would seek elsewhere in vain. The combination gives evidence of irrecusable value as a source of material for a study of the years preceding the Revolution. Artists, *amateurs* of the theater, historians and literary historians, sociologists, and the mere curious would not regret making an excursion into the eighteenth century, into the many and varied milieux of the closing decades of the Ancien Régime, with Carmontelle as cicerone. The domain through which the former *lecteur* of the Duke of Chartres would guide them is vast and fecund in surprises.

JAMES B. WHITLOW

THE SHIP CYCLE IN
LES FLEURS DU MAL

Despite Baudelaire's admonition that *Les Fleurs du mal* "is not a mere collection of verse and that it has a beginning and an end,"[1] not enough serious attention has been given to the thematic and narrative unity of the work as a whole. In studies of its architecture, critics have emphasized the a posteriori arrangement which Baudelaire made of the poems by theme, subject, and the mistresses whom he extolled; but these critics fail to point out more than a tenuous connection between the beginning and the end of the book. According to Marcel Ruff, an intensive analysis of the order and arrangement of the poetry would remain conjectural since "the poems were not conceived for the place assigned to them."[2] Henri Peyre has expressed a similar view and concludes that more important for study than the architecture of the whole work is that of the individual poems "taken in isolation, in their internal order."[3] And Marcel Françon, still less affirmative, raises doubts as to the logical unity of the volume.[4]

It is evident that the disposition of the poems alone does not immediately give them the coherence which Baudelaire might have wished. My purpose in this paper is to call attention to the poetic imagery as an equally crucial factor of unity, and, in particular, to one key symbol, that of the ship, whose cyclical recurrence not only confirms the meticulous care with which Baudelaire is supposed to have ordered his material, but serves to unify the various themes implied in the titles of the book's six divisions.

145

It is in the first division, called "Spleen et Idéal," that the most frequent uses of the ship image occur. Near the beginning of this section, in poems inspired for the most part by Jeanne Duval, the poet describes in some detail his imaginary voyages to a tropical Eden. The physical attributes of Baudelaire's mistress constantly evoke in him reveries of a marine paradise where he envisions a seaport and sailing vessels, as for example in these lines from "Parfum exotique":

> Guidé par ton odeur vers de charmants climats,
> Je vois un port rempli de voiles et de mâts
> Encor tout fatigués par la vague marine. . . .[5]

Similarly, in "La Chevelure" the poet sees himself transported upon the "dark ocean" of his mistress's hair to a distant shore of ideal warmth and beauty where he delights in the contemplation of ships gliding in and out of port. His personification of a ship embracing "the glory / Of a pure sky" reveals his own feelings towards this world of imagination.

The repeated imagery of these poems not only indicates a strong associational pattern of ideas in the mind of the poet, it also serves to strengthen the symbolic values of the images themselves. Thus, in the voyage reverie, the ship is equated with the poet; the sea, primarily identified with his mistress, symbolizes more especially the dream stimulus; and the imagined paradise is the object of the poet's abiding nostalgia for an ideal world of luxurious ease where "tout n'est qu'ordre et beauté / Luxe, calme et volupté" (FM, LIII).

The meanings of the three images, however, are sometimes interchanged. In "Le Serpent qui danse," for example, an almost ritualistic departure is maintained in the beginning of the poem, and the usual symbolic values are attached to the ship-sea-Utopia cluster:

> Sur ta chevelure profonde
>   Aux âcres parfums,
> Mer odorante et vagabonde
>   Aux flots bleus et bruns,
> Comme un navire qui s'éveille
>   Au vent du matin,
> Mon âme rêveuse appareille
>   Pour un ciel lointain.
>   (FM, XXVIII)

But in the seventh stanza, the graceful rolling movement of a ship is employed to suggest the rhythmic stride of Jeanne Duval:

> Et ton corps se penche et s'allonge
> Comme un fin vaisseau
> Qui roule bord sur bord et plonge
> Ses vergues dans l'eau.

These purely descriptive lines appear to be a continuation of the idyllic mood which we have already noticed. However, an ambivalence has been added in the characterization of the beloved. Whereas in previous instances of the ship image (e.g. "La Chevelure," "Parfum exotique"), the poetic mood was completely lyrical, here the symbolism strikes a first discordant note of evil. The very title of the poem announces that the beloved is a dancing serpent. It is also worth while observing that the "odorous sea" of Jeanne's hair has a sharp scent, that her cadenced walk is that of a wanton beauty, and that the heavenly ecstasy which she generates is both bitter and overpowering. And in "Le Beau navire," where she is again compared to a sailing vessel and to a serpent, she is pictured in the medieval rôle of temptress, with powers of black magic to enhance her sinister charms.

But the added complexity of these poems, obtained through contrasting images of beauty and evil, does not affect the aesthetic basis of the ship image itself: rhythm and harmony remain the dominant qualities. Commenting on the fascination which the ship held for Baudelaire, Henri Peyre observes that in the complicated rhythm and gentle swaying of a ship Baudelaire found "that harmony which governs a very broad ensemble, a movement both steady and self-controlled, which he likes to find in everything that captivated him and in which we are inclined to see the very symbol of Baudelaire's art."[6] The poet himself has given us his analysis of the ship's aesthetic appeal:

I believe that the mysterious and infinite charm found in the contemplation of a ship, and especially a ship under sail, lies in the first place in its rhythm and symmetry, which are primary needs of the human mind . . . ; and in the second place, in the successive increase and proliferation of all the imaginary curves and shapes drawn in space by the real elements of the object.[7]

While it is certainly true that the ship was for Baudelaire an admirable aesthetic symbol, it is also true that in his poetry it stands for much more. The poems dealing with euphoric reverie or with physical beauty united to evil, such as the pieces we have looked at, are later followed by "Moesta et errabunda," a poem in which the ship becomes the symbol of liberation from the actual world of suffering and moral corruption. Here the poet's plea to be delivered from the "foul city" introduces a negative motif into the voyage theme:

> Emporte-moi, wagon! enlève-moi, frégate!
> Loin! loin! ici la boue est faite de nos pleurs!
> (FM, LXII)

Yet, as before, there is the familiar pining for an imaginary paradise of sensuous pleasures and childhood innocence—a world which now seems so remote in time and space that Baudelaire asks if it can be recalled once more and brought to life:

> —Mais le vert paradis des amours enfantines,
> L'innocent paradis, plein de plaisirs furtifs,
> Est-il déjà plus loin que l'Inde et que la Chine?

This question is partly answered in what might be taken as the second stage of the spiritual journey, represented by "La Musique" and "L'Héautontimorouménos." Instead of enjoying the marvelous Edenic visions of past days, the poet must confront the "tempests of passion" and the "calm sea of despair." It is notable that as the ocean assumes its archetypal rôle of hostility to human goals, there is an ever closer identification of the ship with the poet. In the first of the two poems, his body, having been metamorphosed into the bow and sails of a ship, is able to experience directly the sensations of a "vessel that suffers"; in the second poem, he is seen as a ship sailing upon a "sea of tears." Here Baudelaire's emphasis on suffering, and especially his moral deviation into sadomasochism, reveals the desperation of his attempts to escape from his "Saharah," an allusion not only to the spiritual apathy of *ennui*, but also to the spiritual desert of contemporary society. His failure to escape from this desert and to reach the "green paradise" of his dreams is implied in the contrasting symbolism of the bitter "sea of tears" wrung from his mistress and the life-giving water struck from the desert rock by Moses.

The plight of the poet-ship now bears a reminiscence of a passage in the prose poems where Baudelaire speaks of "a little sail shudder-ing on the horizon which by its smallness and isolation imitates my irremediable existence."[8] The present voyage cycle, however, moves on to its culmination in the long poem titled "L'Irrémédi-able." Here the function of the ship image is all the more important because this poem is the actual conclusion to the section "Spleen et Idéal". The "irremediable" fortune described in the poem is that of a soul fallen into Hell, and is indicated by five symbolic sketches: "an idea sunken / Into the muddy Styx" locates the scene in a Dantesque Inferno; "an Angel, an imprudent voyager who was tempted by love of discord" reminds us of the disgrace of Lucifer; "a bewitched wretch" and "a damned soul descending / The edge of the abyss" once more suggest the horrors of the Inferno; finally, the reappearance of the ship, trapped at the bottom of the abyss, calls to mind the fate of Satan himself:

> Un navire pris dans le pôle
> Comme en un piège de cristal
> Cherchant par quel détroit fatal
> Il est tombé dans cette geôle. . . .
> (FM, LXXXIV)

These five symbolic figures, which mirror the poet's own destiny, emphasize not only his misery in Hell, but also his quandary at being there and the hopelessness of his getting out. Since the ship immobilized in the ice of the Inferno is certainly to be identi-fied as the same ship which had set out earlier for a heavenly paradise, the present odyssey indeed ends on a note of tragic irony.

What remains to the soul irremediably damned? In contempla-tive detachment, it sees itself as in its own mirror and discovers there one consolation: the consciousness of evil. Though permeated with "Satanic grace," this knowledge of guilt would seem to bring the sinner at least partial atonement, were it not for the fact that in his morally conscious humanity he finds not merely consolation for his sins, but "his only glory." Through this act of self-exaltation, rather than of humility and contrition, the consciousness of Evil becomes caught in a perpetual cycle of spiritual pride and damnation. Thus, consistent with the parallel destinies of the ship and Satan is this final image of Baudelaire as an unregenerate sinner.

In the second division of *Les Fleurs du mal,* Baudelaire shifts his attention from the introspective "tableau of an irremediable fate" toward the objective world. The result is another genre of tableau: the "Tableaux parisiens." But just as the charms of Baudelaire's mistress at the beginning of "Spleen et Idéal" called forth the imagery of the ship, together with an imaginary voyage and a vision of utopian felicity, so does the City, at the beginning of "Tableaux parisiens," evoke both the ship image and the dream of another Eden. Through a characteristic associative process, the City, too, becomes a vision of a ship, and the "masts of the city," perceived from a garret window, await only the will of the poet to set sail for an imaginary paradise.

> Et quand viendra l'hiver aux neiges monotones,
> Je fermerai partout portières et volets
> Pour bâtir dans la nuit mes féeriques palais.
> Alors je rêverai des horizons bleuâtres,
> Des jardins, des jets d'eau pleurant dans les albâtres,
> Des baisers, des oiseaux chantant soir et matin,
> Et tout ce que l'Idylle a de plus enfantin.
>
> (FM, LXXXVI)

This urban "eclogue" demonstrates the poet's ability to conjure up visions of an idyllic childhood in a renewed effort to find a poetic refuge against the imperfections of earthly existence. Plunged in what he calls the *"volupté /* Of evoking Springtime through my will," he can remain unaffected by the strife taking place in the external world.

Nevertheless, Baudelaire is always compelled to return from dream to the real world that lies about him. Paradoxically, however, the Paris of reality (like T. S. Eliot's London) turns out to be a "City peopled by dreams." The poet is startled by a hallucinatory world of specters. And in "Les Sept vieillards," the apparition of seven identical ghosts causes a complete breakdown of his reason. What is important to note here is that Baudelaire's reaction to the mystery and absurdity of the seven old men is expressed in the metaphor of a storm-imperiled ship *(vieille gabarre):*

Vainement ma raison voulait prendre la barre;
La tempête en jouant déroutait ses efforts,
Et mon âme dansait, dansait, vieille gabarre
Sans mâts, sur une mer monstrueuse et sans bords!
(FM, XC)

Like the final occurrence of the ship image in "Tableaux parisiens," the example just cited of a ship in dire peril invites comparison with the disaster which finally overtakes the ship at the end of the preceding section. Especially noteworthy is the associative pattern of imagery which links once again the ship's disaster with the idea of Hell. In the present instance, the poet is shaken by the "infernal" aspect of the seven ghosts, who come "all from the same hell." Their demonic origin may be one reason why the old men have been identified with the seven capital sins. But we may surmise also that, as deathlike wanderers in Baudelaire's wasteland, they represent in a more general sense man's denial of God, including, of course, the poet's own.

The transgression that is most commonly, but not always most accurately, associated with *Les Fleurs du mal,* has to do with sexual perversions. The fourth division of the book, also called "Fleurs du mal," treats the subject, but centers particularly on the *chercheuses d'infini* who, contemptuous of reality, aspire to the absolute through the flesh. It is not surprising that one of the major poetic statements in this chapter is called "Un Voyage à Cythère." This allegory reiterates the voyage themes with which we are now familiar. The poem opens on a note of anticipated bliss reminiscent of Watteau's "Embarquement pour Cythère." But as the ship approaches the isle of Venus, the disillusionment of the passengers on board turns to shock at the sight of a curious object which proves to be not a temple of Love, but a gibbet. Thereon, a human victim is seen being destroyed by vultures. In a typical Baudelairean movement, the perspective of the poem shifts from the objective presentation of scene to the poet's identification of himself with the victim. Thus, all the major ingredients of the previous voyage patterns—the imaginary paradise, the voyage to a deserted wasteland, the Promethean fate of the poet (a parallel to the fall into Hell)—are combined in the allegory of carnal love.

But the poem which gives us the most complete synthesis of Baudelaire's spiritual journey is itself titled "Le Voyage." A highly significant poem in many ways, it not only ends the book, but it adopts, like the prologue, "Au Lecteur," a more philosophical tone than do the majority of the pieces. Although the poem is essentially about death, the poet is led to review in the same symbolic terms the voyage of life. Baudelaire classifies life's voyagers into four categories, each of which is represented by one or more poems that we have seen: the fugitives who rejoice in escape ("Moesta et errabunda"); the "real voyagers," who dream of attaining unknown *voluptés* ("L'Invitation au voyage"); the sedentary voyagers who delight in imaginary voyages ("La Chevelure"); the disconsolate, such as the Apostles or the Wandering Jew, for whom nothing will avail in their attempt to flee the burden of Time ("Les Sept vieillards").

Whether impelled by the negative desire of escape or the positive motive of curiosity, all voyagers have one purpose in common: they all aspire to the infinite:

> Et nous allons, suivant le rhythme de la lame,
> Berçant notre infini sur le fini des mers. . . .
>   (FM, CXXVI)

But the term *volupté*, with its connotations of sensuality, is constantly used by Baudelaire to translate the infinite. The infinite is even associated with *orgie;* it is equated with the intoxication of the Lotus; and it is the goal of those who take refuge in opium, or any of the dream stimulants of the poet's *Paradis artificiels.* The geographical counterpart of *volupté* is a land whose name suggests an earthly paradise. Hence, the human soul is compared to a ship seeking one of these paradises: "Notre âme est un trois mâts cherchant son Icarie. . . ." In spite of their promise of happiness, all of the intellectual or physical pleasures sought within the finite world cannot appease those restless souls who demand limitless satisfaction. And whether it be called Icaria, Eldorado, Capua, or China, the Zion of reverie is never reached. The world of reality always betrays the dream. What the voyagers finally attain is the symbolic opposite of their ideal: a barren reef, the abyss of Hell, a hovel, all types of human vice, and always ennui and human evil.

Although the voyage of life seems absurd, it is man's very nature never to abandon the search for perfect rest:

. . . L'Homme, dont jamais l'espérance n'est lasse,
Pour trouver le repos court toujours comme un fou!

This renewed aspiration is the key to the many voyages which we have examined. Its recurrence in "Le Voyage" signals the beginning of yet another cycle. In terms of the imagery, then, the voyages of life and death are the same. And as the poet embarks on the ship of Death, he experiences, as he did on previous voyages, the joyful excitement of a younger passenger. To those who know already "the great malady of the horror of one's domicile,"[9] this elation of departure may appear foolish and naïve. But it has become by now ritualistic and is combined with worldly indifference as to the final destination—Heaven or Hell:

O Mort, vieux capitaine, il est temps! levons l'ancre!
Ce pays nous ennuie, ô Mort! Appareillons!
Si le ciel et la mer sont noirs comme de l'encre,
Nos coeurs que tu connais sont remplis de rayons!

Verse-nous ton poison pour qu'il nous réconforte!
Nous voulons, tant ce feu nous brûle le cerveau,
Plonger au fond du gouffre, Enfer ou Ciel, qu'importe?
Au fond de l'Inconnu pour trouver du *nouveau!*

The poet sailing once again is wiser because of his former experiences. The destination of his voyage remains equivocal; yet, the motive of this unique journey remains unchanged: the quest for an absolute which all of the artificial paradises of this world cannot bring.

RIMA DRELL RECK

FLAUBERT'S ARTISTIC WAGER

"I AM BENT furiously over my work. . . . What I do is for myself, for myself alone, like playing a game of dominoes so that life will not be too unbearable."[1] Gustave Flaubert described his devotion to the craft of literature in these words in his *Correspondance*, letters spanning the years 1830 to 1880 and constituting a document which may be his greatest single literary work. Intense work was Flaubert's remedy for the nauseating state of *le monde actuel* and the external set of circumstances which he found totally unacceptable. Tracing Flaubert's artistic journey from the age of nine years to the time of his death, the *Correspondance* is a voluminous unpolished chronicle of thoughts and events paralleling the small, infinitely careful literary opus.

From the boy who dreams of writing plays, of creating *une œuvre,* to the sensitive young man turning further in upon himself as his contempt for the society of his time grows, to the older artist mourning the death of friends and watching his world shrink, the *Correspondance* reveals consistent preoccupations. A hatred of "normal life" and a refusal to be a participant or a dupe of it are accompanied by a deepening immersion in the practice of literature. "Furious with myself, I tore out the man with both hands. . . . From this green tree I wanted to make a naked column, so that I could place at the very top, as on a altar, some sacred flame" (IV, 234).

The doctrine of "art for art's sake" was natural to Flaubert. A tendency at first, only later it became a program. The artist "refined

154

out of existence, paring his fingernails," whom Stephen Daedalus describes in *Portrait of the Artist as a Young Man,* is perhaps the twentieth century's distorted image of Flaubert as a man unconcerned, detached, infinitely godlike and serene. The *Correspondance* reveals instead a tormented romantic temperament trying obstinately to reveal none of his sensibilities in prose, hoping rather to extirpate his lyricism in the rhythms of banality and monotony demanded by his chosen subject matter.

Impassibility and style are the key concepts of Flaubert's aesthetics. They define an artistic attitude and draw up standards for a craft. We shall examine the meaning of these terms as revealed in the *Correspondance* in order to shed some light on the function of literature both for the artist and for the future of art itself. In an era which finds so many French writers unable to justify literature unless it has social and political functions, Flaubert's stance seems a deliberate defiance. And yet, in the light of his special view of the world, it may well be that his was the most responsible attitude of all, a dedication to his art beyond the temporal passions of the majority of his contemporaries.

I. The Approach to the Idea: Impassibility

Flaubert's inherent desire for permanency in things and in people was constantly frustrated; he turned to what he called the "Ideal." "The Ideal consoles you for the Real" (V, 280). The only constant he seemed able to find in life was illusion. "I believe in the eternity of only one thing, that of Illusion, which is the fundamental truth. All the others are merely relative" (II, 51). And yet the artist was unable to accept baldly this truth of which he remained convinced; he sought a means of mediating between illusion and the ideal, artistic creation. The practice of "art in itself" became a consolation for and a reconstitution of what immediate experience failed to provide (V, 378).

It would be incorrect to understand Flaubert's involvement in art as an indication of his certainty that art was the only, the sure answer to his dilemma. He recognized his commitment as an *arbitrary* occupation. In answer to a friend who begged him to seek publication and wide recognition, Flaubert replied:

In this life you preach to me, I would lose the little I have; I would assume the passions of the crowd in order to please it, I would descend to its level. Just as well remain by one's fireside, doing Art for oneself alone, as one plays at ninepins. Art, in the final analysis, is perhaps no more serious than a game of ninepins. Everything is perhaps nothing more than an immense joke; I am afraid, and when we shall be on the other side of the page, we shall perhaps be quite astonished to learn that the key to the riddle was so simple (II, 329).

Rather than the certainty that he had chosen the right path, that the pursuit of perfection in art was the only worthwhile dedication of one's life, Flaubert saw his choice as one among others, a choice subject to error and liable to reveal in the final summing up the one thing he most feared, that he had wasted his life. He stressed repeatedly the gamelike aspect of art for art's sake, the sense of staking all he had on a result he could not foresee. Flaubert's dedication to his craft was a kind of wager, in which he might win or lose, but in which the *choice* itself was sufficient to fill a man's life with totally absorbing work.

"There are now only two ways of living for the *pure ones*: either to bury your head in your cloak . . . or else to raise yourself to such a level of pride that no splashings of mud from the outside can reach you" (III, 50). The "furious work" Flaubert chose in response to the banality of his era was for him both a defense and a source of pride and pleasure. At times he called writing "a torture," but the letters reveal constantly that he delighted in its agonies. The artist's role was for him the highest; the practical labor involved was preferable to all other activities.

The artistic attitude of impassibility, "an infinite and hidden impassibility," has frequently been understood as a complete dis-interestedness on Flaubert's part. This interpretation tends to distort Flaubert's basic intention. He wrote, "The author in his work must be like God in his creation, invisible and all-powerful; one must feel him everywhere, but one must not see him" (IV, 164). Impassibility is not detachment; on the contrary, it is a special kind of involvement, in some ways deeper and more perilous than the blatant authorial intrusion characteristic of many of Flaubert's predecessors. He admitted that the novelist has no right to express any opinion, for does God give his opinion (V, 253)? But, "he can communicate it" (V, 396). Rather than a completely detached description of reality, impassibility is a fuller mode of vision, one which attempts to free the artist from reality's hold in order to give him greater power to grasp it. In this connection, one letter from the *Correspondance* merits extensive quotation.

If I had a more solid brain, I would not have become ill from study-ing law and being bored. . . . Sorrow, instead of resting in my brain, ran down into my limbs and bent them into convulsions. It was a kind of *deviation.* There are some children whom music makes ill; they have great talents, remember melodies at first hearing, become exalted playing the piano, their hearts beat, they grow thin and pale, fall ill, and their poor nerves, like those of dogs, twist with suf-fering at the sound of the notes. These are not the Mozarts of the future. The *vocation* has been displaced; the idea has passed into the flesh where it remains sterile, and the flesh perishes; there results neither genius nor health.

The same thing in art. Passion does not make verses, and the more you are personal, the more you are weak. *I* have always sinned in that direction, myself; it's because I have always put my-self into everything I've done. In the place of *Saint Antoine,* for example, I am there; the *Temptation* was for me and not for the reader. *The less you feel a thing, the more likely you are to express it as it is* (as it is *always* in itself, in its generality and detached from all its ephemeral contingencies). But you must have the ability to *make yourself feel it.* This ability is nothing other than genius: *to see,* to have before you the model which poses (II, 461–62).

The innately romantic Flaubert sought to channel his sensibility in a productive direction. The youthful illness of which he spoke, his epilepsy, has been the subject of extensive studies, medical as well as literary. It is not our aim here to debate the effect of the disease on his literary output. What is significant for an understand-ing of Flaubert's conception of impassibility is the physical analogy he employed. He sensed that extreme involvement in things and in passions could be a deterrent to literary communication. One is naturally reminded of Wordworth's definition of poetry as "emotion recollected in tranquillity." James Joyce, who was in many ways a disciple of Flaubert, described the highest form of literature, the dramatic, as one in which the author's passions no longer stand visibly between the reader and the work. Flaubert was perhaps the most eloquent spokesman for artistic objectivity Western literature has seen to date. More striking in this respect than Oscar Wilde, whose intoxication with his public image detracted considerably from his artistic tenets, Flaubert remained determined to penetrate the shell of appearance in pursuit of reality, at the expense of his most natural inclinations.

To see the world and its objects as models, to *describe* rather than to be *involved*, these were the goals of the impassible creator. As Benjamin Bart has pointed out, there is a special kind of Platonism in Flaubert's position.[2] But Professor Bart stresses unduly perhaps the beneficent function of art pursued in Flaubert's manner as a means of moving men. It was first of all and above all a personal struggle for some kind of creative redemption, if we are to believe what Flaubert wrote in the *Correspondance*. Art is the *handling of reality*, a game serious in its moves but hopefully unconcerned about winning since the artist cannot know the outcome. There was evidently *a truth in things* for Flaubert; he went so far as to suggest that things do have an intrinsic immutable nature: "Each thing is an infinite; the smallest pebble is as arresting a thought as the idea of God" (II, 411). But he remained eternally uncertain and fearful. He attempted to divert his attention from the correctness of his speculations to the practice of his art. Like Stendhal, he was anxious not to be a *dupe* of his own inclinations.

Flaubert had very strong feelings and opinions about the world in which he lived, but he expressed them openly only in private letters. Of course, in a sense, every phrase of *Madame Bovary*, *L'Education sentimentale*, and *Un Cœur simple* is a veiled form of criticism. Flaubert sensed two dangers in expressing his reactions publicly. First of all, he would have been subject to ridicule by that "majority of men" he so detested. More important, any definite judgement of *le monde actuel* was of course subject to error, therefore to temporality. To create something enduring one had to shore it up with elements not liable to fashion or to decay. Flaubert wrote, "What form must one find in order sometimes to express his opinion on the things of this world, without running the risk of looking like an imbecile later on? This is a difficult problem. It seems to me that it is best to depict them, simply, those things which exasperate you. To dissect is a vengeance" (V, 347).

Deeply uncertain of the ultimate fate of artistic creation, Flaubert vacillated between a deep concern over what would be found "on the other side of the page" and a desire to be free of involvement.

The artistic attitude of impassibility was the answer to that dilemma. Flaubert speculated that only the artist who would some day have the insight "to write the facts from the point of view of a *superior joke* . . . from on high" would ever achieve the serenity and detachment of God (II, 37). Impassibility was not such a joke; it was indeed elevated, but it was also serious. The impassible artist could take hold of reality without at the same time himself risking dissolution and death. He could combine the vengeance of dissection with the creation of beauty, clearly, for him, the aim and the basic characteristic of art. Flaubert believed that impassibility would enable him to be creature and creator at once, the judged and the judge, that he would be able to depict all things, yet remain immune from suffering the experience of all things:

When one wishes, great or obscure, to meddle with the creations of the Lord, one must begin . . . by being in a position not to be fooled. You will be able to depict wine, love, women, glory, on the condition . . . that you are not a drunkard, nor a lover, nor a husband, nor a foot-soldier. Involved in life one doesn't see it very well; one suffers or enjoys too much. The artist, in my view, is a monstrosity, something outside of nature (II, 268–69).

The impassible artist is more than a man; he is a special kind of creature whose relation to the world is at once more intimate and more detached than the normal one. A kind of greedy sensuality is apparent in Flaubert's confessions of pleasure experienced while writing. He enjoyed the dissection; by elaborating the characteristics of the monuments to bad taste he saw around him, he served the ideal of beauty. But perhaps more fundamental was the pleasure of Flaubert the man at being able to stretch his world far beyond the limits of Croisset and occasional trips to Paris and the Middle East. He wanted *more* than the life of any one man could offer. In one of the most beautiful of his letters Flaubert described the writing of the love scene between Emma Bovary and Rodolphe:

Good or bad, it's a delicious thing to write, to no longer be *oneself*, but to circulate in everything one describes. Today for example, man and woman together, lover and mistress at once, I rode horseback in a forest on an autumn afternoon, under yellow leaves, and I was the horses, the leaves, the wind, the words they spoke and the red sunlight which made them half close their eyelids heavy with love. In this pride or piety, is it the naïve overflowing of an exaggerated sense of oneself? or instead a vague and noble instinct of religion? But when I think of those pleasures after having experienced them, I am tempted to render up a prayer of thanks to the good Lord, if I knew he could hear me. Let him then be blessed for not having made me be born a cotton merchant, vaudevillist, a man of sense, etc. (III, 405).

The artist is a special kind of monster, one who aspires to be a god. However, he cannot fully achieve this position; the final certainty, so desperately desired, is never assured. "The stupidity lies in wanting to conclude. We are a thread and we want to know the woof" (II, 239). Flaubert was aware that the "page" would never be turned over in his lifetime. He was in a sense writing at all times what he believed to be on the other side. At this point the most important aspect of impassibility came into play, its practical application in writing. Flaubert's doctrines of style in literature provided the position of omniscience to a man worried by an unproved certainty. The style of the impassible artist gave him absolute power in a limited domain. He attempted to find *within his very medium,* in the words and the way they were used, the complete universe of which he could be undisputed master. Concentrating on the physical act of writing, Flaubert made his struggle with reality depend not on the ultimate meaning of what he wrote, but on the concrete way he used his tools. The doctrine of artistic impassibility underlies all Flaubert's ideas of style, form, and judgment of the work of art.

II. Style as a Mode of Vision

"The Fact is distilled in the Form and rises on high like a pure incense of the Spirit toward the Eternal, the Immutable, the Absolute, the Ideal" (III, 407). Flaubert firmly believed that the immutable reality in *things* could only be approached through form, which is the most concrete, the least uncertain element in literature. The Idea is expressible only in carefully considered usage of the matter of literature, the words. The following is typical of the advice he gave to aspiring writers who sought his direction: "Think more, then, before writing and attach yourself to *the word.* All the talent of writing consists after all only in the choice of words. The precision makes the force. With style as with music, what is most beautiful and most rare is the purity of sound" (II, 471). Flaubert felt that words should be used not to produce emotional effects, as had been the case during the Romantic movement, but to capture and delineate as closely as possible reality, which embodies the Idea. He sought "not the *vibration* but the *design*" (II, 72). In capturing concisely the outline, the appearance of reality, Flaubert felt he would simultaneously penetrate "the Idea," the content. "The form and the idea, for me, are one and I do not know what one is without the other" (IV, 243). But by the idea, the content, he did not mean subject matter. For Flaubert the content of a work of art was in the way it revealed the artist's mode of thought and of seeing. "The more an idea is beautiful, the more the phrase is sonorous. . . . The precision of thought makes (and is itself) that of the word" (IV, 243).

Any attempt to separate the idea from the style in which it is expressed was a total misunderstanding in Flaubert's view, "a sophism. Everything depends on the conception" (II, 339). Style in literature is merely another name for the way of seeing. He wrote, "Style is only a manner of thought. . . . The style is as much *beneath* the words, as *in* the words. It is the soul as well as the flesh of a work" (IV, 315).

Originality of style, therefore, is originality of vision. In a letter to Baudelaire expressing his admiration for *Les Fleurs du mal*, Flaubert wrote, "The phrase is all filled with the idea, to the bursting point" (IV, 205). Flaubert admitted that he himself *felt* a great deal more than he *said* in his writings, because he put all emphasis on the style. His impassibility was a way of distilling his vision into the very substance of his sentences. The *Correspondance* is filled with impatient outcries against the difficulty of writing impassively, against the hateful subjects Flaubert had chosen. The documentation of reality involved hard work for him, quite different in kind from the note-taking obsessions of the Goncourt brothers. Things in the world did not simply "pose"; they had to become part of "the artist's interior vision." The process as Flaubert described it resembled a form of hallucination, with the difference that instead of loss of personality the writer experienced a form of joy unalloyed by terror. "Something passes before your eyes; that's the moment you must fling yourself upon it" (III, 350).[3]

But Flaubert's greatest desire was to become less dependent on interior vision and on documentation of reality. His ultimate ideal of style was one in which the style would become the very movement of thought itself. In the following letter, he spoke of the ideal book, one with no subject, a book about nothing.

What seems beautiful to me, what I would like to do, is a book about nothing, a book with no external attachment, one which would hold together alone by the internal force of its style, just as the earth stays in the air without being held up, a book which would have almost no subject or at least where the subject would be almost invisible, if that is possible. The most beautiful works are those where there is the least matter; the more the expression approximates the thought, the more the word sticks to it and disappears, the more beautiful it is. I believe that the future of Art is in this direction. . . . When it is skilful, form is softened; it abandons all liturgy, all rules, all measures; it abandons the epic for the novel, verse for prose; it recognizes no orthodoxy and is as free as each will which produces it. . . .

For this reason there are no good and no bad subjects and one could almost establish as an axiom, from the standpoint of pure Art, that there are no subjects, style being unto itself an absolute manner of seeing things (II, 345–46).

In addition to eloquent statements of the independence of art, Flaubert had many practical ideas on the writing of prose. Most commonly known, of course, is his demand for *le mot juste*. However, there was much more involved than simply the choice of apt descriptive terms. Sated with humanitarian eulogies, sentimental outbursts, antiquarian modes, violently opposed to *le mot commun* which debilitated the prose of many of his contemporaries, Flaubert called for a new prose: "Let it be clear as Voltaire, tufted as Montaigne, nervous as La Bruyère and always, shimmering with color" (II, 434). In the letters of specific stylistic criticism on manuscripts sent him by friends and admirers, Flaubert always spoke to the language itself, the correctness of word usage, the aptness of a phrase, the transitions between sections. He simply pointed out to others the things he worked at in his own writing. "Style . . . is a thing I take to heart. . . . What a strange mania is this, to spend one's life wearing oneself out over words and sweating all day long to round out sentences" (II, 53).

Flaubert sought to perfect the art of prose and bring it to the stylistic level and the conciseness of poetry. He was convinced that poetry had for all practical purposes reached its end as a mode of expression appropriate to his era. He conceived an ideal prose which would combine the finest elements of all previous forms of literature with the basic aims of impassible art, in order to create the art of the future: deep and exacting psychological and historical observation coupled with perfection of language. A good prose sentence, according to Flaubert, would be as inalterable, as rhythmic and sonorous as a line of poetry. He was aware that no one before him had ever dreamed of a more perfect form of prose (II, 468). The ultimate aim of such a prose style would be a literary form of *truth*.

I love art. There at least everything is freedom in this world of fictions. There you satisfy everything, you do everthing. . . . Humanity is a puppet with bells that you make ring at the end of your sentence like a juggler with the end of his foot. . . . How the burdened soul unfolds in this azure which stops only at the frontiers of Truth. Where the Form is lacking, the idea is no more. . . . To seek one is to seek the other. They are as inseparable as substance is from color and for this reason Art is truth itself (II, 415–16).

As Flaubert understood it, art for art's sake was an eminently moral enterprise. The artist achieves a much desired certainty within the limits of his self-created context. But within that context, he has obligations and labor to perform. "Art must not be a plaything. . ." (V, 178-79). Art accepts existence ironically and re-creates it plastically. Politics, morality, philosophy, people are thus *manipulated*. This is partial vengeance for the fact that the artist cannot determine them.

Throughout Flaubert's letters one finds expressed a fear of conclusions and a skepticism about results. As far as he could determine, the sciences began to make rapid progress only when they abandoned the idea of ultimate causes and devoted themselves to observation and experimentation. "I know of nothing more noble than the ardent contemplation of the things of this world. Science will become a faith. . . . But for this, we must come out of our old scholastic habits: not make these divisions of form and content, body and soul, which lead nowhere;—there are in the Universe only facts and groups of facts" (IV, 357). In such a universe, style is the only possible morality for the artist. The impassible artist does not judge because he knows the futility of judgment: if he judges wrongly his work will be valueless, and he can never know if he has judged rightly. Therefore, the only possible moral defense of a work of art is its truth: "the moment a thing is true, it is good" (II, 428). This was the one "elevated pyramid with a solid base" Flaubert could find in mid-nineteenth-century France. "The moment you prove, you lie. God knows the beginning and the end; man, the middle" (II, 380).

If we recall that in 1857 both Flaubert and Baudelaire were hounded by the law for the evil subject matter of their respective works, Flaubert's frequent invocations of "Truth" can be seen as reactions to a depressingly moralistic era in French life. It is at times difficult for a modern reader to imagine that most of Flaubert's readers believed "that beautiful subjects make good books"; to them the author of a novel about adultery, as unattractive as that sin may appear from the fate of the heroine, was an immoral man who preached adultery. Little wonder that Flaubert wrote in a letter, "Oh the public! At times when I think of it, I feel for it one of those immense and powerless hatreds, as when Marie Antoinette saw the Tuileries invaded" (II, 219–20). He admitted that his reluctance to publish what he wrote was a way of hiding from a public he held in contempt. "The moment you publish, you descend from your work" (II, 384–85). Flaubert made a conscious unpopular choice when he decided to write according to untried standards. He found himself isolated, little read and much vilified. His "ivory tower" dedication was a mixture of pride and fear. Flaubert had made a wager on the future of literature.

They work to overthrow some minister who will fall without them, when they could, by one line of satirical verse, make his name eternally opprobrious. They worry about taxes, import duties, laws, about peace and war! How small all that is! How all that passes! How all that is false and relative! . . . It is much finer, it seems to me, to go the distance of several centuries to make the hearts of generations beat and fill them with pure joys (I, 321–23).

III. A Literature of Transition

"The great geniuses . . . don't have to worry about style . . . they are powerful in spite of all their faults and because of them. . . . Great men often write quite badly, and so much the better for them.

That is not the place to look for the art of form, but in the second rank (Horace, La Bruyère). One must learn the masters by heart, idolize them, try to think like them, and then separate oneself from them forever" (III, 31–32). Flaubert was painfully aware, despite his unshakable conviction that his contemporary judges were idiots, that he belonged to the second rank of literature. He recognized few "great geniuses": Shakespeare, Cervantes, Michelangelo, Homer, Rabelais, Goethe. His own era, he felt, was inherently inimical to the birth of any literary giants.

One of the greatest weaknesses of the art for art's sake movement, in Flaubert's eyes, was precisely its broadmindedness. "We have wide tastes because we admit everything and we try to place ourselves at the point of view of the object in order to judge it. But do we have as much of what is innate as we do of understanding? Is a ferocious originality even compatible with so much breadth?" (II, 218). He recognized that geniuses were frequently narrow-minded and immune to qualities unlike their own. And Flaubert confessed that the eclecticism of the enlightened artists of his era might well be the mark of their inferiority. Of course, he preferred an enlightened inferiority to the utter stupidity of what was popular in his time. One thought consoled him: "Beauty is not compatible with modern life" (V, 260).

While maintaining an unwavering defense of his "private pursuit" of art, Flaubert had a broad view of the function of literature in his unprivileged era. He saw himself and his fellows as a sort of bridge or intermediary stage in the development of art. "*We* came either too early or too late. We shall have accomplished what is most difficult and least glorious: the transition. To establish something lasting, one needs a firm base; the future torments us and the past holds us back. That's why the present eludes us" (II, 279). It is apparent that Flaubert, one of the great theoreticians and defenders of the art for art's sake movement, had no real illusions about the sufficiency of his literary position. A rapidly changing material and political world around him, a shifting point of view in the sciences, these uncertainties fostered his natural inclination to withdraw from the world. The hermit of Croisset railed against the public whose taste he despised, but deeply envied those epochs in the past when artists were closer to their audiences. Most deeply, he felt the lack of a fixed goal for the "furious work" he had chosen as a way of life:

The public is so stupid! And besides, who reads? And what do they read? And what do they admire? Ah! fine tranquil eras, good eras with wigs on, you lived upright on your high heels and your canes! But the earth trembles under us. . . . What we all lack is not style, nor that flexibility of the bow and the fingers called talent. We have a large orchestra, a rich palette, varied resources. In the matter of tricks and strings, we know much more than perhaps anyone ever knew. No, what we lack is the intrinsic principle, the soul of the things, the very idea of the subject. We take notes, we travel; misery, misery. We become scholars, archeologists, historians, physicians, cobblers, and men of taste. What does all that add? Where are the heart, the verve, the sap? Where to leave from and where to go? (II, 202).

The transition artists, in which group Flaubert counted himself, were in fact superior technicians of the art of literature, savants of style who had little to say, but knew how to say it exquisitely. However individually painful their role might be, as products of their era they deserved attention. The appreciation of their contributions to the future of art required critics attuned to the new literature and capable of judging it fairly. For this end, Flaubert dreamed of a criticism practiced like natural history, "without a moral idea" (III, 367). The old standards of proper form for each literary genre could not possibly be sufficient to the understanding of a new style. Art itself would tend, in the future, to approach the objectivity of the sciences; for such an art a new criticism had to arise.

The primary demand Flaubert made of criticism was that it treat the new literature in its own terms. He considered writing a work of literary criticism himself, a series of "Prefaces" in which he planned "to make evident why aesthetic criticism has remained so far behind historical and scientific criticism: *they had no basis for judgment*. The knowledge they all lack is *the anatomy of style*, to know how a sentence is put together and what it is attached to" (III, 336-37). Elsewhere Flaubert spoke of the "physiology of style" (III, 360), again demanding that the emphasis of the critic be where the emphasis of the writer is. (In his own case, this was of course the style.) Flaubert refused on the surface to concern himself with moral and social questions. He viewed the study of history as no more than a curious collection of disparate data. And he had little patience with critics who treated literature from any of these perspectives. "Hasn't modern criticism abandoned Art for History? The intrinsic value of a book is nothing in the school of Saint-Beuve and Taine. They take everything into consideration, except talent" (VI, 295). However, Flaubert did not admire the other extreme of criticism, which saw the work of art as a gift from the gods. In the following letter to George Sand, he commented on her admiration for Taine:

Taine's *English Literature* interests you. His work is lofty and solid, although I do not approve of its point of departure. There is something else in Art besides the milieu in which it is practiced and the physiological antecedents of the practitioner. With that system, you explain the series, the group, but never the individuality, the special fact which makes one be *that one*. This method forcibly leads you to take no account of *talent*. The masterpiece no longer has any meaning except as a historical document. That is the radical opposite of the old criticism of La Harpe. Then, they believed that literature was a completely personal thing and that works fell from the sky like meteors. Now, they deny all will, any absolute. The truth lies, I think, between the two (V, 160).

Above all, Flaubert reproached critics like Sainte-Beuve and Taine for their presumption in *drawing conclusions*. "No great genius concluded and no great book concludes, because humanity itself is always moving and it does not conclude. Homer does not conclude, nor Shakespeare, nor Goethe, nor the Bible itself" (IV, 183). According to Flaubert the ideal criticism would be concerned with the work in itself, its origin, composition, style, and the author's point of view. The only possible mediation between a mediocre era and the artist's eternal thirst for beauty lay perhaps in giving to criticism as well as to art "the precision of the physical sciences" (IV, 164). Flaubert realized with pathos that "beauty will perhaps become a feeling useless to humanity and Art will be something halfway between algebra and music" (III, 18).

The impassible artist, beneath his apparent scorn for the future and for "conclusions," actually longed for certainty. For Flaubert the strongest hope for the future of art lay in a scientific direction. "The further it goes, the more Art will become scientific, just as science will become artistic" (II, 395). His doctrine of style was, in a sense, a gesture toward the glorious time to come when art and science would meet at the pinnacle of the pyramid. But Flaubert's gesture was always restrained by his doubts of what would be found on "the other side of the page." And he felt most sharply the futility of being an artist isolated in his era, "in a corridor full of shadows" (II, 395). Having made his wager on the future of art in his novels, he tried to minimize the seriousness of his enterprise and its far-reaching consequences:

From the crowd to us, no link. So much the worse for the crowd, so much the worse for us above all. But since each thing has its reason, and since the whim of an individual appears to me as legitimate as the appetite of a million men, and it can have as much importance in the world, one must, abstracting things and independently of the mass which denies us, live for one's vocation, climb into one's ivory tower and there, like a bayadere in her perfumes, remain alone in our dreams (II, 396).

NOTES

August W. Staub

1 Allardyce Nicoll, *World Drama From Aeschylus to Anouilh* (London, 1949), 796.
2 Laurence LeSage, *Jean Giraudoux, Surrealism, and the German Romantic Ideal,* Illinois Studies in Language and Literature, Vol. XXXVI, No. 3 (Urbana, 1952), 5.
3 Joseph Wood Krutch, *Modernism in Modern Drama* (Ithaca, N.Y., 1953), 12.
4 Percy Lubbock, *The Craft of Fiction* (New York, 1957), 251.
5 E. M. Forster, *Aspects of the Novel* (New York, 1954), 79 ff.
6 Leon Edel, *The Psychological Novel, 1900–1950* (New York, 1955), 85.
7 Helen Gardner, *Art Through the Ages* (New York, 1948 edition), 734.
8 Martin Lamm, *Modern Drama* (New York, 1953), 113.
9 *Eleven Plays of Henrik Ibsen* (Modern Library Edition; New York), xi.
10 Alan S. Downer, *The Art of the Play* (New York, 1955), 315.
11 For a full discussion of the Kaiserian New Man see William Harlan Shaw, *German Expressionism, 1915–1920: The Plays of Georg Kaiser* (Ph.D. dissertation, Louisiana State University, 1955).

Donald G. Schueler

1 The exception, the Seventh Book, contains an encyclopedic introduction to a wide variety of subjects.
2 *Complete Works of John Gower,* ed. Georgie C. Macaulay (4 vols.; Oxford, 1901–1902), I, xxxvi–vii. Book and page numbers in text are from this edition.
3 And as Macaulay and W. G. Dodd have said they are. *Works,* II, xix, and *Courtly Love in Chaucer and Gower* (Gloucester, 1959), 73.
4 With this difference: the vision is a "day-dream." The Lover is awake when he wanders into the allegorical landscape.
5 It is the inevitable, two-fold operation of this natural law—passion on the one hand and age on the other—which drives the Lover, at poem's end, to the refuge of God.

170 — Notes to Pages 22–38

6 Cf. Peter Fison's "The Poet in John Gower," *Essays in Criticism,* VIII (1958), 16–26.
7 Macaulay (ed.), *Works,* II, xvii.

RAEBURN MILLER

1 *The Edinburgh Review* (April, 1848), 422, quoted in Horace Howard Furness (ed.), *A New Variorum Edition of Shakespeare: A Midsummer Night's Dream* (New York, 1963), 305.
2 What finer image could be found than the one Shakespeare provides to show the nature of Theseus? One would expect his relations with Hippolyta and his use of the wood for reasonable ends to be sufficient, but Shakespeare adds for us the description of his hounds:

> Slow in pursuit, but matched in mouth like bells,
> Each under each. A cry more tuneable
> Was never holloaed to nor cheered with horn
> In Crete, in Sparta, nor in Thessaly.
> (IV. i. 122–25)

Theseus has lifted even the fierceness of hunting dogs to the rational level of harmony and art.

COOPER R. MACKIN

1 This and all subsequent passages are quoted from *The Works of John Milton,* ed. Frank A. Patterson, *et al.* (21 vols. and index vol.; New York, 1931–42).
2 Leo Spitzer, *Classical and Christian Ideas of World Harmony: Prolegomena to an Interpretation of the Word "Stimmung,"* ed. Anna Granville Hatcher (Baltimore, 1963). First published in *Traditio,* II (1944), 409–64; and III (1945), 307–64.
3 Spitzer, *Classical and Christian Ideas of World Harmony,* 35, 48.
4 Jackson I. Cope believes that this scene is illustrative of Milton's pervasive use of paradox. See "Time and Space as Miltonic Symbol," *Journal of English Literary History,* XXVI (1959), 503–504; reprinted in *The Metaphoric Structure of Paradise Lost* (Baltimore, 1962), 58–59.
5 Spitzer, *Classical and Christian Ideas of World Harmony,* 50. Adam and Eve are "lulld by Nightingales" before the fall (IV, 771).
6 Prolusion II, "On the Harmony of the Spheres," in *Complete Prose Works of John Milton,* ed. Don M. Wolfe, *et al.* (New Haven, 1953), I, 237.
7 See especially Book IX, 670–76, and cf. the final lines of the prologue to Belial's speech in Book II, 117–18: ". . . he pleas'd the ear, / And with perswasive accent thus began."
8 Satan's unnatural use of voice to effect the downfall of mankind is given a richer perspective when read against the background of the Invocation to Book III, 7–12:

> Or hear'st thou rather pure Ethereal stream,
> Whose Fountain who shall tell? before the Sun,
> Before the Heavens thou wert, and at the voice
> Of God, as with a Mantle didst invest
> The rising world of waters dark and deep,
> Won from the void and formless infinite.

Chaos, responding to God's creating voice, becomes ordered; with their sin, Eve and Adam metaphorically return us to the "formless infinite."

9 This image is traceable to Book III of the *Aeneid,* where the Harpies are characterized by discordant noise.

10 The association of tempests with evil spirits was commonplace: see Kester Svendsen, *Milton and Science* (Cambridge, Mass., 1956), 99–100.

11 Brilliantly demonstrated by Professor Cope in Chapter IV of *The Metaphoric Structure of Paradise Lost,* "Scenic Structure in *Paradise Lost.*"

SERAPHIA LEYDA

1 The autobiographical aspect of Shelley's heroes is so general an assumption in most critical studies that a full consideration of that aspect of the poetry would require greater space than is possible here. It is not my purpose in this article to add to the already lengthy commentary on that subject.

2 *Alastor, or the Spirit of Solitude,* ll. 75–77, p. 18. All quotations from Shelley's poetry and prefaces, as well as Mrs. Shelley's notes, are from *The Complete Poetical Works of Percy Bysshe Shelley,* ed. Thomas Hutchinson (London, 1961). Line references or page numbers are given in the text.

3 See Carlos Baker, *Shelley's Major Poetry: The Fabric of a Vision* (New York, 1961), 47, for corroboration of this reading. See also A. C. Bradley, *Oxford Lectures on Poetry* (London, 1909), 152–53.

4 *Alastor* is posited as a first step toward the final apocalypse of *Adonais* by Ross Woodman in *The Apocalyptic Vision in the Poetry of Shelley* (Toronto, 1964), which is, in part, a convincing application of De Rougemont's "Tristan Myth" of Death and Eros to Shelley's poetry. My conclusions are quite different from those drawn by Mr. Woodman.

5 See Peter Butter, *Shelley's Idols of the Cave* (Edinburgh, 1954), 8.

6 For a review of the longstanding problem of an apparent discrepancy between the preface and the poem see Baker, *Shelley's Major Poetry,* 42–47.

7 See Olwen Ward Campbell, *Shelley and the Unromantics* (New York, 1924), 190; Raymond D. Havens, "Shelley's *Alastor,*" *PMLA,* XLV (1930), 1100.

8 Compare with the famous "dedicatory" lines, 31–36, in *The Revolt of Islam,* and also the song of the Spirits in *Prometheus Unbound,* II, iii, 93–99.

9 This reading of *Athanase* departs from the opinion of critics from Stopford A. Brooke to Ross Woodman. See for example: Stopford A. Brooke, *Poems of Shelley* (London, 1887), 322; A. Clutton-Brock, *Shelley, The Man and the Poet* (London, 1923), 125; Ellsworth Barnard, *Shelley's Religion* (Minneapolis, 1937), 275; Floyd Stovall, *Desire and Restraint in Shelley* (Durham, N.C., 1931), 151.

10 Newman Ivey White, *Shelley* (2 vols.; New York, 1940), II, 533–36; Carl Grabo, *The Magic Plant: The Growth of Shelley's Thought* (Chapel Hill, N.C., 1936), 175–76.

11 See Edmund Blunden, *Shelley, A Life Story* (New York, 1947), 211.

12 *Epipsychidion* was not, of course, the last of Shelley's love poems; however, it is so obviously the culmination of a pattern which began with *Alastor* that I have treated it as such.

13 See for examples Algernon Charles Swinburne's "Note on *Epipsychidion*" in *Epipsychidion,* ed. Robert Potts, Facsimile Reprint, Shelley Society (1887); Floyd Stovall, "Shelley's Doctrine of Love," *PMLA,* LXV (1930), 301; Archibald T. Strong, *Three Studies in Shelley* (London, 1921), 124.
14 See Barnard, *Shelley's Religion,* 281.
15 See Richard Harter Fogle, *The Imagery of Keats and Shelley* (Chapel Hill, N.C., 1962), 229–30.
16 Denis de Rougemont, *Love Declared: Essays on the Myth of Love* (Boston, 1964), 224.
17 For other interpretations see Stovall, *Desire and Restraint,* 276–77; Baker, *Shelley's Major Poetry,* 234; Butter, *Shelley's Idols of the Cave,* 17–19.

GEORGE F. REINECKE

1 Albert J. Guerard, *Conrad the Novelist* (Cambridge, Mass., 1962), 272–73 and notes; also Thomas Moser, *Joseph Conrad, Achievement and Decline* (Cambridge, Mass., 1957); and Douglass John Hewitt, *Conrad, A Reassessment* (Cambridge, 1952).
2 Guerard, *Conrad the Novelist,* 272–79.
3 Joseph Conrad, *Victory* (Garden City, 1957), ix–xvi. I have used this Anchor paperback reprint by the original American publisher as the most easily accessible form of the novel and therefore the most appropriate for page references. Future references are given in the text, designated by *V.*
4 Letter to Richard Curle of March 3, 1913, published in *Conrad to a Friend* (Garden City, 1928).
5 Jocelyn Baines, *Joseph Conrad* (New York, 1960), 447, quoting a letter to Conrad's friend Garnett.
6 Baines, *Joseph Conrad,* 447.
7 Joseph Conrad, *A Personal Record* (New York, 1912), 150.
8 This horizontal and vertical scheme was first suggested to me in somewhat different form in a very able paper by a former undergraduate at Louisiana State University in New Orleans, Mr. Gerald Tassin, whom I take this occasion to thank.
9 Paul L. Wiley in his *Conrad's Measure of Man* (Madison, Wis., 1959), 15, remarks, "As the reader becomes familiar with [Conrad's] works, the images that he is likely to remember most vividly are those which can be described as cosmic or creational within Biblical definition. The background in many of the finest tales is given depth by metaphors of order and chaos, world destruction and rebirth, Last Judgment and Deluge." Wiley is one of the ablest of the upholders of the symbolic view of Conrad.
10 My thanks to Dr. G. Falconeri of the University of Oregon for information pertaining to Chinese language and philosophy.

MALCOLM O. MAGAW

1 *The Confidence-Man: His Masquerade,* ed. Elizabeth S. Foster (New York, 1954); pagination for all subsequent citations from *The Confidence-Man* is from this edition and will be included in the text.
2 In his description of this particular confidence man Melville does, however, include a touch of white imagery. He speaks at one point of the stooped man's "turning up the whites of his eyes" (131).

3 I am indebted to James E. Miller, Jr., for this significant observation; see *"The Confidence-Man:* His Guises," *PMLA,* LXXIV (March, 1959), 104.
4 See Elizabeth S. Foster, "Introduction," *The Confidence-Man: His Masquerade* (New York, 1954), xlix.
5 At least one critic, Richard Chase, strongly denies that the confidence man represents "man" on any level: "Above all, the significant thing about the confidence man is that he is not a man; the perpetually shifting mask never quickens into the features of a human being. His supreme act of confidence is his refusal to accept the full implications and responsibilities of manhood." "Melville's Confidence Man," *Kenyon Review,* XI (1949), 125.
6 As a formalistic critic, I find greater validity in the last of these three positions, of course.
7 See Foster, *The Confidence-Man: His Masquerade,* xc; pagination for all subsequent citations from Miss Foster's essay will be included in the text.
8 Merlin Bowen, *The Long Encounter* (Chicago, 1960), 116.
9 Miller, *"The Confidence-Man:* His Guises," 102.
10 On the basis of these statements and many more, Miss Foster argues that the deaf-mute is, in fact, not one of the confidence men. "Melville clearly differentiates between him and the Confidence Men," she remarks; "he is innocent of fraud; he is unequivocal; he is not on the Negro's list of Confidence Men. Also, Melville clearly seems, in this scene and the next, to be contrasting Christ and Antichrist, to be showing how the devil makes use of Christian idealism for his own ends. The crippled Negro with his 'black fleece,' coming immediately after the lamblike man with his white, fleecy vesture, suggests a deliberate contrast between the pure ideal of Christianity and the black use made of it by the powers of evil, or the white ideal and the black perversion wrought by man" (p. lii).

Since I do not interpret *The Confidence-Man* as a Christian allegory on good and evil, I cannot agree with Miss Foster's thesis. The masks worn by all the confidence men—and I would certainly include the deaf-mute—are in my judgment too ambiguous to be evaluated conclusively as representative of good or evil. The meanings imputed to them by the passengers are illusory and subjective. Melville leaves their final meanings undefined: what they appear to be to men may or may not be what they really are. Thus, despite his apparent singularity, the deaf-mute could be as much an illusion as any of his successors. From this point of view he is indeed one of the confidence men. But even on the simpler narrative level he is a confidence man, for he is seeking men's confidence in the Christian doctrine of love.
11 See Miller, *"The Confidence-Man:* His Guises," 105–106.
12 See St. Luke (chs. xxii–xxiii) and St. John (chs. xviii–xix).
13 Richard Chase, *Herman Melville* (New York, 1949), 187–88, *n.*

WILLIAM E. DOHERTY

1 Maxwell Geismar, *The Last of the Provincials* (Cambridge, Mass., 1947), 333.
2 F. Scott Fitzgerald, *The Crack-Up* (New York, 1956), 298.
3 F. Scott Fitzgerald, "Tender Is the Night, A Romance," *Scribner's Magazine,* XCV (January–June, 1934), 7.
4 Geismar, *The Last of the Provincials,* 290–91.

5 F. Scott Fitzgerald, *Tender Is the Night* (New York, 1962), 40. Quotations in the text are from this edition unless otherwise indicated.
6 Malcolm Cowley, "Introduction," *Tender Is the Night* (New York, 1956), xvii.
7 Albert Guerard, Jr., "Prometheus and the Aeolian Lyre," *Yale Review,* XXXIII (March, 1944), 495.

KENNETH HOLDITCH

1 John Dos Passos, *One Man's Initiation—1917* (New York, 1922), 36. Subsequent references will be included in text, designated *OMI.*
2 Malcolm Cowley, *After the Genteel Tradition* (Gloucester, 1959), 168–70.
3 Letter from John Dos Passos to author, Westmoreland, Va., March 7, 1961.
4 John Dos Passos, *First Encounter* (New York, 1945), 9. Subsequent references will be included in text, designated *FE.*
5 The symbolic value of cathedrals here obviously discredits the assertion of Alfred Kazin that the novel is no more than the "very boyish and arty memoir of a young architect-poet" whose chief complaint is the fact that he cannot admire the cathedrals because of the guns. See Kazin, *On Native Grounds* (New York, 1942), 346–47.

DOROTHY BRATSAS

1 Stéphane Mallarmé, "The Faun," *Stéphane Mallarmé: Poems,* trans. Roger Fry (New York, 1951), 81.
2 Bernardo Couto Castillo, "Las nupcias de Pierrot," *Revista Moderna,* II (enero, 1899), 2, 13. Translations from the Spanish are mine.
3 The following are the last three Pierrot stories: "El gesto de Pierrot," *Revista Moderna,* II (noviembre, 1899), 2, 326; "Caprichos de Pierrot," *Revista Moderna,* III (octubre, 1900), 1, 300; and "El Pierrot sepulturero," *Revista Moderna,* III (mayo, 1901), 142. Couto Castillo's story, "Caprichos de Pierrot," contains fragments of Baudelaire's poem, "Letanias de Satán," translated from the French by Antenor Lezcano. The story is accompanied by several illustrations created by Julio Ruelas, a young painter much admired and respected by the *Revista Moderna* group. Ruelas was the art editor of the magazine and the majority of the cover illustrations were credited to him. His artistic endeavors were in the traditional Romantic style of the period and indicated no noticeable change in technique comparable to that of his literary friends.
4 "El Pierrot sepulturero," *Revista Moderna,* III (mayo, 1901), 142. This story was the last published by Couto Castillo. He died May 3, 1901, a few days before the story went to press. These facts were reported in the same issue in which the story was published.
5 Arthur Rimbaud, "Le Bateau Ivre," *An Anthology of Modern French Poetry,* ed. C. A. Hacket (New York, 1954), 53.
6 Ciro B. Ceballos, "El viejo fauno," *Revista Moderna,* II (abril, 1899), 4, 118. Synesthesia does not appear as often in the *cuento* or *novela* as it does in the *crónica* and poetry of these authors. Their most poetically conceived and executed prose is to be found in the *crónica.* In this genre there is a great transference of poetic technique.
7 José Juan Tablada, "El dios de Netzahualcoyotl," *El Mundo Ilustrado,* XVI (septiembre, 1905). [This issue is not paginated.]

8 Carlos Díaz Dufóo, "El primer esclavo," *Revista Azul*, I (3 junio 1894), 70–71.
9 Díaz Dufóo, "El primer esclavo," 70.
10 J. J. Tablada, "Exempli Gratia," *Revista Moderna*, I (julio, 1898), 2–3.
11 Tablada made his trip to Japan in 1900–1901, Rebolledo his in 1906.
12 Efrén Rebolledo, *Hojas de bambú* (Santiago, Chile, 1926).
13 Ernesto Leduc died in 1908 and Bernardo Couto Castillo in 1901.
14 Efrén Rebolledo, *Saga de Sigrida la blonda* (Kristiania, 1922).
15 *Ibid.*, 108.
16 J. J. Tablada, *La resurrección de los ídolos*. (Mexico, 1924).
17 J. J. Tablada, "Cuentos a Umbria," *Revista Moderna*, I (1 diciembre 1898), 143.

MARIE LAGARDE

1 *Mémoirs secrets pour servir à l'histoire de la République des lettres depuis MDCCLXII jusqu' à nos jours, ou Journal d'un observateur* par feu M. de Bachaumont (Londres, 1767), XVIII, 82.
2 *Souvenirs du baron de Frénilly (1768–1828)* (2e édition; Paris, 1908), 6.
3 Frénilly, *Souvenirs*, 6. All translations from the French are mine.
4 *Proverbes et comédies posthumes de Carmontel* (Paris, 1825), I, i.
5 *Allgemeines Lexikon der Bildenden Künstler*, begründet von Ulrich von Thieme und Felix Becker (Leipzig, 1912), VI, 15–17.
6 Pierre Lièvre, "Proverbes de Carmontelle, à la Comédie-Française," *Mercure de France*, CCLXXXIV (15 mai 1938), 151–55.
7 *Correspondance littéraire, philosophique et critique*, par Grimm, Diderot, Raynal, Meister, etc. (Paris, 1881), IX, 264.
8 Sainte-Beuve, *Causeries du lundi* (IIIe édition; Paris, 1858), III, 536.
9 Carmontelle, *Proverbes dramatiques* (Paris, 1773), I, vii.
10 Carmontelle, *Proverbes dramatiques*, I, vii.
11 Frénilly, *Souvenirs*, 7.
12 Victor du Bled, *La Comédie de société au XVIIIe siècle* (Paris, 1893), 1–2.
13 Eugène Lintilhac, *Histoire générale du théâtre en France* "La Comédie, dix-huitième siècle" (Paris, 1909), IV, 25.
14 *Ibid.*, IV, 27.
15 Bachaumont, *Mémoirs secrets*, III, 16 février, 1768.
16 *Ibid.*, XIX, 280–81.
17 Grimm, *Correspondance littéraire*, IX, 263–64.
18 *Nouveaux Proverbes dramatiques* (Paris, 1811), I, ix.
19 Frénilly, *Souvenirs*, 6.
20 Carmontelle, *Conversations des gens du monde dans tous les tems de l'année* (Paris, 1786), I, i.
21 Sébastien Mercier, *Tableau de Paris* (Amsterdam, 1783), II, 255–56.

JAMES B. WHITLOW

1 *Correspondance générale* (6 vols.; Paris, 1947–53), IV, 9.
2 *Baudelaire* (Paris, 1955), 105.
3 *Connaissance de Baudelaire* (Paris, 1951), 70–71. All translations from the French are mine.
4 "L'Unité des Fleurs du mal," *PMLA*, LX (1945), 1132–33.
5 Baudelaire, *Fleurs du mal*, in *Œuvres complètes* (Paris: Pléiade edition,

1954), 100. All subsequent references to *Les Fleurs du mal* are to this edition and are given in the text as numbered in the collection.

6 "L'Image du navire chez Baudelaire," *Modern Language Notes*, XLIV (1929), 449.

7 *Journaux intimes*, in *Œuvres complètes*, 1201.

8 *Le Spleen de Paris*, in *Œuvres complètes*, 284.

9 *Journaux intimes*, in *Œuvres complètes*, 1217.

RIMA DRELL RECK

1 Gustave Flaubert, *Correspondance* (9 vols.; Paris, 1926-33), II, 355. All references to the correspondence are to this edition and are given in the text. Translations from the French are mine.

2 Benjamin F. Bart, "Flaubert's Concept of the Novel," *PMLA*, LXXX (March, 1965), 84–89.

3 In this letter, written to Hippolyte Taine, Flaubert spoke of the poisoning of Emma Bovary. "My imaginary characters *affect me*, haunt me, or rather *I* am in them. When I wrote the poisoning of Emma Bovary, I had so strong *a taste of arsenic in my mouth*, I was so thoroughly poisoned myself that I became sick twice. . . ."

CONTRIBUTORS

Dorothy Bratsas, assistant professor of Spanish at Louisiana State University in New Orleans, received her Ph.D. from the University of Missouri in 1963. She is at work on a monograph entitled *Decadence: One Aspect of the Expression of Modernism in Mexican Prose.*

William E. Doherty, formerly instructor of English at Louisiana State University in New Orleans, received his Ph.D. from Tulane University in 1965. He is presently an assistant professor of English at the University of Illinois at Chicago Circle and is at work on a book dealing with the novels of George Moore.

Kenneth Holditch, assistant professor of English at Louisiana State University in New Orleans, received his Ph.D. from the University of Mississippi in 1961. He has published an article in *The Explicator* and short stories in *Phylon, Delta Review,* and *Watauga Review.*

Marie LaGarde, associate professor of French and acting chairman of the Department of Foreign Languages at Louisiana State University in New Orleans, received her Ph.D. from Tulane University in 1956. She is currently at work on articles on Musset and Carmontelle and on a monograph about Charles Testut.

Seraphia Leyda, assistant professor of English at Louisiana State University in New Orleans, received her Ph.D. from Tulane University in 1965. She has published an article in the *Louisiana Folklore Journal* and is working on a study of Shelley.

Cooper R. Mackin, associate professor and chairman of the Department of English at Louisiana State University in New Orleans, received his Ph.D. from Rice University in 1962. He has published an article in *Studies in Philology*, reviews in *College Composition and Communication, Choice: Books for College Libraries*, and *Books Abroad*, and is preparing a book on the poetry of John Oldham.

Malcolm O. Magaw, assistant professor of English at Louisiana State University in New Orleans, received his Ph.D. from Tulane University in 1964. He has articles forthcoming in the *Bucknell Review* and the *University Review*, and is at work on a study of Melville.

Raeburn Miller, assistant professor of English at Louisiana State University in New Orleans, received his M.F.A. at the University of Iowa in 1960. He has numerous poems published or forthcoming in the *Paris Review*, the *Southern Review, Beloit Poetry Journal, Western Humanities Review, International Literary Annual*, and others.

Rima Drell Reck, associate professor of French and Comparative Literature at Louisiana State University in New Orleans, received her Ph.D. from Yale University in 1960. She is associate editor of the *Southern Review* and has published articles on modern literature in *Yale French Studies, Modern Drama, French Review, University of Kansas City Review, Modern Language Quarterly, Criticism, Forum, James Joyce Quarterly, Southern Review, Books Abroad*, and others. Her translation of Giraudoux's *Paris Impromptu* appeared in the *Tulane Drama Review*. She is at work on a study of literature and responsibility in the twentieth-century French novel.

George F. Reinecke, associate professor of English and chairman of the departmental committee on graduate study in English at Louisiana State University in New Orleans, received his Ph.D. from Harvard University in 1960. He has published articles and reviews in *CEA Critic, Louisiana Folklore Miscellany*, and *Louisiana English Journal*. He served as editorial assistant to Fred Norris Robinson in the preparation of the second edition of the *Works of Geoffrey Chaucer*, and his critical edition of Lydgate's *St. Alban and St. Amphibalus* will appear shortly in the Early English Text Society Series with Oxford University Press.

Donald G. Schueler, associate professor of English at Louisiana State University in New Orleans, received his Ph.D. from Louisiana State University, Baton Rouge, in 1962. He has published an article in the *Louisiana English Journal*, a book on programmed English, and is preparing a monograph on John Gower.

August W. Staub, associate professor and chairman of the Department of Speech and Theater at Louisiana State University in New Orleans, received his Ph.D. from Louisiana State University, Baton Rouge, in 1960. He has published numerous articles in the *Quarterly Journal of Speech* and the *Southern Speech Journal*. He is presently preparing a text on play direction to be published by Harper & Row.

James B. Whitlow, instructor of French at Louisiana State University in New Orleans, received his M.A. from the University of Chicago. He is preparing his doctoral dissertation on Baudelaire for Stanford University.

LOUISIANA STATE UNIVERSITY STUDIES

THE STUDIES WAS established to publish the results of research by faculty members, staff, and graduate students of the University. Manuscripts of exceptional merit from sources other than aforementioned are considered for publication provided they deal with subjects of particular interest to Louisiana.

The Studies originally appeared as a unified series consisting of forty-two numbers, published between the years 1931 and 1941. In 1951 the Studies was reactivated, and is now being issued in the following series: Social Sciences, Humanities, Biological Sciences, Physical Sciences, and Coastal Studies. Other series may be established as the need arises.